SOFTWARE FOR ARTISTS BOOK

Edited by Zainab Aliyu and organized with The School for Poetic Computation. Published on the occasion of Software for Artists Day 2023, by Pioneer Works Press.

#003
IN POETIC COALITION

Ayana Zaire Cotton is an anti-disciplinary worker from Prince George's County, Maryland. Based in Dawn, Virginia—tucked in between the ancestral lands of the Mattaponi and Youghtanund—they are answering the call to steward land that has been in their family for four generations. Ayana recently founded Seeda School, a skill-building platform for learning how to code through a black feminist lens, where she publishes a newsletter and podcast titled *Soft, Where?*. Through the ecosystem of their practice Ayana braids abstraction, teaching, and world-building to engage our collective imagination around the technologies we need in the world we desire.

Yatú Espinosa and Norm O'Hagan are artist-founders of Teal Process & Company and have recently been careering via Fill in the Blank Inc. by playing with USBs.

Neema Githere (b. Nairobi, Kenya) is a writer, artist, and guerrilla theorist whose work explores love and indigeneity in a time of algorithmic debris. Having dreamt themselves into the world via the internet from an early age, Githere's work prototypes relationality-as-art through experiments that span curation, community organizing, social design, travel, and image-making. Githere is a 2023–24 Practitioner Fellow at the Digital Civil Society Lab at Stanford University, where they are working on a project entitled "Data Healing: A Call for Repair."

Dorothy R. Santos (she/they) is a Filipino American storyteller, poet, artist, and scholar. Her work has been exhibited at Ars Electronica, Rewire Festival, Fort Mason Center for Arts & Culture, Yerba Buena Center for the Arts, and the GLBT Historical Society. Her writing appears in *art21*, *Art in America*, *Ars Technica*, *Hyperallergic*, *Rhizome*, *Slate*, and *Vice Motherboard*.

Eileen Isagon Skyers is a writer, curator, and artist based in New York. She has worked across non-profit and contemporary arts institutions including David Zwirner, Rhizome, and the Whitney Museum of American Art. Through her experience with web3 organizations including Foundation, Feral File, and FWB, Skyers has facilitated high-profile partnerships with distinguished collaborators including bitforms gallery, Almine Rech, MoMA, LVMH, ARS, Uniswap, and Topical Cream. Her critical writing on digital art and culture has been published in *Hyperallergic*, *Outland*, *Frieze*, and *Dirt*, among others, and in printed catalogs including Rhizome's *Net Art Anthology* and *Trigger: Gender as a Tool and Weapon*.

Lynne Yun is a NYC-based type designer, educator, and technologist. Lynne is a co-founder of Space Type, a studio practice operating at the intersection of type and technology. She also recently co-founded Type Electives, an online design school shaping the future of type. Lynne has the honor of having served on the board of AIGA NY and worked as a full-time type designer for Monotype. She holds a BFA in graphic design from the School of Visual Arts, a postgraduate certificate in typeface design from Type@Cooper, and an MPS from New York University's Interactive Telecommunications Program.

Or Zubalsky is an artist and educator based in Lenapehoking (Brooklyn). They explore how interactive systems shape socio-political relations and the ways in which coding participates in practices of resistance. Zubalsky is a research engineer at Art.coop and part-time faculty at Parsons School of Design where they teach in the Design and Technology BFA and MFA programs. They are currently a NEW INC incubator member in the Art and Code track and a Pioneer Works technology resident.

American Artist makes thought experiments that mine the history of technology, race, and knowledge production, beginning with their legal name change in 2013. Artist is a recipient of the Herb Alpert Award in Visual Art and a Creative Capital grantee. They are alumn of the Whitney Museum Independent Study Program and have exhibited at the Museum of Modern Art; Whitney Museum; Studio Museum in Harlem; Kunsthalle Basel, Switzerland; and Nam June Paik Center, Seoul. Artist is a co-director of the School for Poetic Computation and a core faculty at Yale School of Art.

Shani Peters (b. 1981, Lansing, Michigan) is a multi-disciplinary artist based in New Orleans, Louisiana. She holds a BA from Michigan State University and an MFA from the City College of New York. Peters has presented work in the US and abroad at the New Museum; the Schomburg Center for Research in Black Culture in Harlem; Seoul Art Space Geumcheon in South Korea; the National Gallery of Zimbabwe; and the Bauhaus Dessau. She is a co-director of The Black School, an artist-initiated experimental art school that is presently working to build a physical home for its art education and community programming in New Orleans's Seventh Ward.

Sam Lavigne is an artist and educator whose work deals with data, surveillance, cops, natural language processing, and automation. He is currently an assistant professor in the Department of Design at UT Austin.

rahel aima is a writer, editor, and critic in Dubai. She is editor of *BXD: The Postwestern Review*, a consulting editor at *Momus*, and was the founding co-editor of *THE STATE*. She is currently at work on a collection of essays about the Khaleeji lowercase ideology, techtopian environmentalism, and where oil meets water in the Arabian Gulf.

Allie Linn is a curator, artist, and arts administrator engaging with alternative institution-building, site-responsive practices, and queer kinship. They hold an MFA in Curatorial Practice from MICA, where they have also taught as a visiting professor, and work as Initiatives Manager at United States Artists, where they oversee Shift Space, an online publication reflecting on the field of art and technology. They have previously held positions at Recess, The Contemporary, Analog Research Lab, Gormley Gallery, and the Baltimore Museum of Art, alongside various artist-run projects and programs, including Bb, a collaborative storefront project space in Baltimore from 2014 to 2016.

Kameelah Janan Rasheed was born in East Palo Alto, California. Rasheed lives and works in Brooklyn, New York. A learner, she grapples with the poetics-pleasures-politics of Black knowledge production, information technologies, [un]learning, and belief formation. Most recently, they are a recipient of a 2022 Schering Stiftung Award for Artistic Research; a 2022 Creative Capital Award; a 2022 Betty Parsons Fellow – Artist2Artist Award from Art Matters; a 2022 Experiments with Google Artists + Machine Intelligence Grant; and a 2021 Guggenheim Fellowship in Fine Arts. Rasheed is the author of four artist books: *i am not done yet* (Mousse Publishing, 2022); *An Alphabetical Accumulation of Approximate Observations* (Endless Editions, 2019); *No New Theories* (Printed Matter, 2019); and the digital publication *Scoring the Stacks* (Brooklyn Public Library, 2021). Her fifth artist book is due out in 2023 from KW Institute for Contemporary Art (Berlin, DE). Their writing has appeared in *Triple Canopy*, *The New Inquiry*, *Shift Space*, *Active Cultures*, and *The Believer*. Rasheed founded Mapping the Spirit, a digital archive documenting how Black faith lives, shifts, and self-revises.

Dana Kopel is a writer and editor living in Los Angeles. As an editor at the New Museum in New York, she helped organize the New Museum Union–UAW Local 2110. She subsequently worked as a staff organizer with the Office and Professional Employees International Union Local 153, helping nonprofit staff unionize. Her writing on art and labor appears in *The Nation*, *The Baffler*, *Frieze*, *SSENSE*, and numerous other publications. Dana is currently a PhD student at UCLA, where she focuses on histories of labor and working-class organizing in the twentieth-century United States.

manuel arturo abreu (b.1991, Santo Domingo) is a non-disciplinary artist who lives and works on unceded lands of Multnomah, Cowlitz, Clackamas, Chinook, Kalapuya, Confedered Grand Ronde people, and other Pacific Northwest First People. abreu works with what is at hand in a process of magical thinking with attention to ritual aspects of aesthetics. Since 2015, they have co-facilitated home school, a free pop-up art school in the Pacific Northwest with a multimedia genre-nonconforming edutainment curriculum.

Coalescing Imminent Possibilities

An introduction by SFPC co-directors Zainab Aliyu, American Artist & Celine Wong Katzman.

This introduction was written in June of 2023.

The words "poetic computation" together generate intrigue. They evoke a structural critique of what constitutes hardware; code written in gratuitous ways; poetry that's programmatic; art that undermines the ubiquity of silicon and coltan. Poetic computation is all of these things: it is a relational practice organized around communal study; an act of resistance against utilitarian notions of efficiency; a colorful theory of culpability.[1] When one shares that they teach at the School for Poetic Computation, everyone does a double take—"what did you say, exactly?" It's a combination of words rarely heard together, inspiring a vibrant community of artists, technologists, and creative practitioners to cultivate an environment where imagination flourishes and new possibilities for creative expression and critical perspectives can emerge.

The School for Poetic Computation (SFPC), founded in 2013,[2] is an experimental platform for the study of these fields of inquiry, among others. SFPC is redefining what it means to be an artist, programmer, student, and teacher by empowering participants to determine their experiences and education, collectively shaping curricula and the school's structure. Through online and in-person classes, events, workshops, residencies, and collaborative projects, we ask: how would our world be impacted by a radical field of computation led by people who are Black, Indigenous, of color, trans, gender non-conforming, queer,

1. Definitions of "poetic computation" by Neta Bomani, Zainab Aliyu, and American Artist. More definitions can be read in the Digital Diaries section at the end of this publication.

2. The School for Poetic Computation was founded in 2013 by Taeyoon Choi, Zach Lieberman, Amit Pitaru, and Jen Lowe.

disabled, survivors, from low-income backgrounds, and of various nationalities and citizenship statuses? Solidarity across social differences, alongside a communal ethic, are grounding forces within the culture of our school.

Most important are intimate moments forged by shared study: the cooking of giant pots of vegetarian stew during class breaks; the welcomed silences alongside the harmonious hums of our hardware; the collective struggling through readings that transform our worldviews; the memes we make together; the relationships built on shared trust, interest, and curiosity that start in the classroom and extend beyond. SFPC is a collective project: dreaming of an ideal learning experience is best done in conversation with others.

In 2020, in the midst of the Covid-19 Pandemic and the ongoing Black liberation movement, a group of students, teachers, staff members, and organizers began advocating for SFPC to make transformations towards becoming a healthier place to study and work. The fifteen people stewarding SFPC during this transition were Zainab Aliyu, Todd Anderson, American Artist, Neta Bomani, Emma Rae Bruml, Luke Demarest, Melanie Hoff, Tiri Kananuruk, Celine Wong Katzman, Taylor Levy, Ashley Jane Lewis, Galen Macdonald, Sebastian Morales, Amber Officer-Narvasa, and Che-Wei Wang. In 2021, we penned a letter to our community[3] which detailed the transition and included a list

3. https://sfpc.study/blog/a-beautiful-school

4. SFPC leadership formerly included Lauren Gardner (2014–20), Zach Lieberman (2013–20) and Taeyoon Choi (2013–21).

5. The School for Poetic Computation's Co-Directors are Zainab Aliyu, Todd Anderson, American Artist, Neta Bomani, Melanie Hoff, Galen MacDonald, and Celine Wong Katzman.

of demands we had made to the former leadership team.[4] We published the demands as an act of accountability for ourselves, and to share our proposal for the beautiful school for transgressive study that we dreamed to work at, so that others might take inspiration from this blueprint. Over two years later, that group of fifteen became the school's now seven co-directors,[5] board members, teachers, and members of the broader community. Together, we began to build the beautiful school proposed by our demands:

1. Actively work towards supporting Black, Indigenous, queer, trans, disabled, and communities of color who are connected by interlocking forms of oppression by dominant systems including but not limited to white supremacy and capitalism.
2. Incorporate critical theory and history into all classes.
3. Have guaranteed need-based tuition, or no tuition at all.
4. Practice radical financial transparency.
5. Protect its workers against economic precarity.
6. Have a cooperative leadership structure.
7. Treat students as collaborators and formally acknowledge the power of students to determine their experience and education.
8. Extend into wider communities and welcome new communities into the school.

9. Actively support our communities by being a genuine platform for grassroots organizing around collective actions.
10. Acknowledge that its members are capable of making mistakes.

These demands have served as a guiding roadmap, leading us towards a vision that aligns with our collective values. It has been more than two years since this letter was published, and we've made several steps in realizing what a beautiful school can be. Since April 2021, we have more than doubled our operating budget and distributed over $150,000 in scholarships, which has had a transformative effect on the accessibility of our education and has allowed us to fundamentally change who is able to study at our school. Remarkably, despite lacking a dedicated physical space, we have managed to maintain a spirited network of community members. Through online classes and in-person classes held in New York City, we have explored subjects such as art, critical theory, software, hardware, and relational ethics. These changes, thrust on us by the pandemic's demand for us to be nimble, have allowed the concept of poetic computation to expand in meaningful ways. Since then, our teachers have taught over thirty classes and these classes have hosted over 400 participants. This viral behavior feels emblematic of our organization's spirit, mirroring the widespread engagement and impact we strive for.

Reflecting on SFPC's storied history in its tenth year, we are excited to welcome our school into its next decade by collaborating with Pioneer Works on Software for Artists Day 2023. Through presentations and writings showcasing distinctive relationships to digital tooling and new technologies, the conference and book series seek to blur the lines that separate artists, technologists, and activists. For this iteration, we invited artists, educators, and labor organizers exploring experimental learning initiatives, many of whom have studied at SFPC, to be in solidarity and conversation with each other.

In a conversation between SFPC alums and artists Neema Githere and Ayana Zaire Cotton, Neema posed the following question: "How do we make love go fractal?"

> I reached this epiphany: it doesn't need to go viral. It needs to go fractal... mimicking this patterning of the forest floor of these root systems and having these frameworks spread in that way. It's inherently emergent and it inherently reaches more people and gets more nutrients to them the same way that mycorrhizal networks do.

During seasonal admissions periods at our school, we often make a reference to the "special sauce" of SFPC—an unspoken quality of our community that is continually reignited and reaffirmed during the start of every new session. The special sauce is what makes SFPC feel the way it does. The realities that many of us want to live and thrive in rely on our "special sauce" fractalizing beyond SFPC. The potential for collective building starts from the small moments of intimacy that bring us together. Artist and educator Or Zubalsky, in his conversation with Sam Lavigne, an artist who teaches at SFPC, speaks about the potential of artists bringing their fluencies to movement spaces and political organizing, and the trust required for this type of collaboration:

> What does that look like, and what kind of technology will support building that sort of trust?... Maybe the technology is just making dinner together.

Our reimaginings of what technology is and can be are at the crux of our school. As writer, artist, and educator Dorothy Santos notes in their conversation with SFPC alum and curator Eileen Isagon Skyers:

> I have hope in it because there are different creators–people coming from different languages and backgrounds–who approach this technology from entirely different perspectives. People forget that we can make magic through technology.

While SFPC focuses on unlearning technologies and our relationships to them, artist manuel arturo abreu explores the potential of rejecting the centering of Western concepts in order to expand our pedagogical pursuits in their essay:

> A network of juxtaposed sources creates a kind of choreography of study; exploring its social components allows for the development of critical perspectives.

These critical lenses inform our ability to move towards defiance of current paradigms. Learner, artist, and SFPC teacher Kameelah Janan Rasheed, in their interview with SFPC alum and writer rahel aima, discusses the potential of building through improvisation, further illuminating the need for responsive institutions that can adapt and collaborate with their engaged participants:

> The hard part for me is thinking about institutions that both have clarity in their values and ethics, while at the same time, being able to hop on a set of caster wheels as necessary. How do we keep the institution in motion? How do we provide opportunities for it to not calcify under the weight of its own values or the weight of its own beliefs about how something is supposed to function?

Similarly, in the pursuit of creating a different model for institutions, artist and educator Shani Peters, in her interview with artist and writer Allie Linn and artist, educator and SFPC co-director American Artist, poses a question to challenge the traditional notion of what a school can be:

> A very big part of what we're trying to do is create a new model. It is institution-building, but institutions don't have to look like the institutions that we've had, so how do we learn and grow and propose something different?

Moving beyond the limitations of institutions to build the futures we dream of inhabiting relies on our collective bargaining power. Writer Dana Kopel highlights the importance of collective action in challenging the constraints of institutions, addressing systemic issues and advocating for change:

> As a worker in an institution... you come up against its limits all the time... The recent museum union movement marks a recognition of this painful truth and a response to it. What we can't accomplish alone, as individuals–livable wages, affordable healthcare, equitable leave policies, a fair process for addressing grievances–we can win collectively.

Lastly, SFPC alum, type designer, and educator Lynne Yun, in her conversation with fellow alums Yatú Espinosa and Norm O'Hagan, describes a dream of overlapping community ecosystems, paving the way for future endeavors to flourish and sustain themselves more easily:

> People often struggle with the idea of starting something new because the first

time doing something is difficult. But hopefully the next time another person wants to start something similar, it'll be easier. Maybe in some years we can sit back and just enjoy all the lovely communities that have sprung around us.

Years from now, we intend to do just that. While we reflect on the years of the school before this moment—its founding and namesake, a massive upheaval, and the hurdles of a new era—we also look towards the next ten years. Our vision for a beautiful school is also one of many beautiful schools; we yearn to see networks in practice of the imminent and otherworldly softly cascading into one another, collectively leveraging the tools we have access to in order to sustainably mobilize together.

SOFTWARE FOR ART-ISTS BOOK

In Poetic Coalition

NEEMA GITHERE & AYANA ZAIRE COTTON

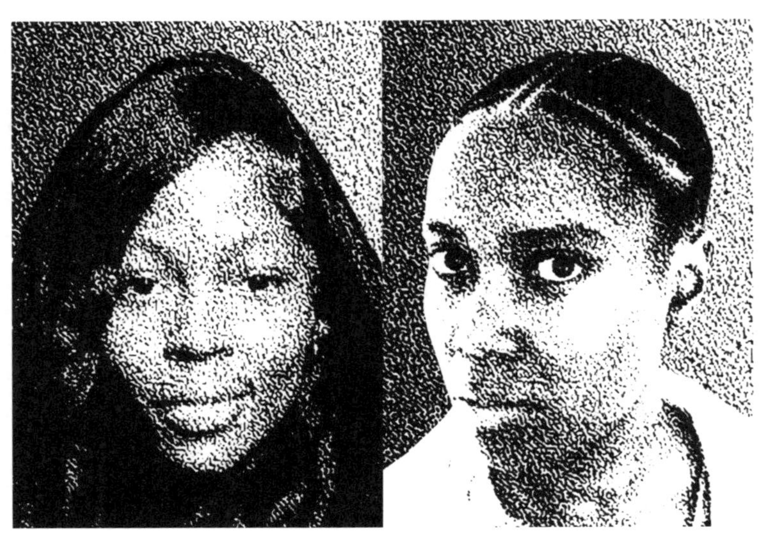

On Making Care Work Go Fractal

Artist and guerrilla theorist Neema Githere in conversation with artist and cultural worker Ayana Zaire Cotton about Black feminist praxis and intuition as technologies for building prototypical learning spaces against the scale of empire.

This conversation between Ayana Zaire Cotton and Neema Githere happened over Zoom in February of 2023. It has been edited for length and clarity.

Neema Githere

Thinking about this theme of world-building and care work, conversation is such a generative way to engage in world-building. To start off, I want to ask you, thinking as expansively as you would like to about the term: what is your favorite technology?

Ayana Zaire Cotton

Whenever I'm talking to folks about technology, I always tell them the first example that I remember seeing was my aunts collaborating in various homes where we would hold family meetings. My aunts would coordinate monthly family meetings when I was growing up and they'd get together and talk about whose house it would be at, who was bringing what. There was one cousin who would do the bookkeeping and folks would pool their money together at each family meeting so that at the end of the year when the holidays rolled around there was an abundance of coin for all of the gift giving for the cousins. I would say that was my first example of seeing Black feminist praxis as technology. And I didn't realize that was my favorite technology until much later.

NG

In Swahili we call that *harambe* when people come together. It's a super common practice here in Kenya, where a group of people will put in a very small amount of money each week or each month and then they rotate each convening who gets to take out of the pot. You do a harambe if somebody has passed on for a funeral or for any major life event you can. Harambe is to come together.

For me, the first one that came to mind is telepathy as an operating system. That feeling when you are really good friends with someone or you're lovers, and you're just really on the same page and you're in a shared space and you both clock something and you just telepathically share a thought. It's the feeling of thinking about someone and then they call you. All the iterations of telepathy that we experience are definitely my favorite because they just remind me that we are just etherically connected, intuitively.

That's my second favorite: intuition as a technology. It's a technology that challenges me sometimes and puzzles me. The best technologies are both very intuitive but also intricate. The right gut feeling is so clear and also so complex to really listen to and put in action because of the interference of doubt and confusion and other signals that you receive. My intuition has been a technology that has always led me, when I allow it, to the most bountiful horizons of my own life. Intuition is a compass. I just love things that God and our ancestors, whatever brought life on Earth, designed for us to allow us to live vividly and meaningfully connect with one another and our environments.

AZC

I've been playing around with this erotic speculation of what would happen if there weren't any screens. If we took away the computer screens, we took away the phone screens, we took away the TV screens… How would we communicate? How would we interact? How would we connect without this hardware that we've developed over the last however long? What I'm hearing you say is intuition is an interface. Intuition as a place of connection, as a portal, as a possibility to replace the hardware that we've surrounded ourselves with. What would it look like to embody the connection that we built all this hardware to stand in the place of? We have all of these servers and all of these cords connecting us physically, like materially, but what would it look like to tap into that telepathy and tap into intuition, those invisible cords, those invisible connectors, those invisible wires that, like you said, we were designed to tap into in some way? It's not there for no reason.

NG

You can't always articulate your intuitive reasoning to somebody else because it's so contextualized by your own needs, conscious or subconscious. We're surrounded by so much artifice, constructed systems and paradigms that do not serve us. In many ways they were designed to subjugate us, to divide us, to make us lose faith in ourselves and one another, and to have us relinquish our agency in service of the state, or in service of commerce. Intuition doesn't care about any of that. Our intuition wants us to be free and that freedom looks so specific to us and our lineage and our needs and its needs. It takes everything to another level because so much of technology as it appears in our lives doesn't encourage that root honesty and root candor. It's just so deeply extractive and disorienting. A lot of my practice stems from trying to confront the feelings of heartache and confusion and disorientation that emerge from always being surrounded by this. It feels very raw because we're told that these technologies and these platforms have our best interests. Sometimes they can, but I don't trust any of them most of the time. Yet, I'm still so deep in all of it.

AZC

A recent theme that I've been noticing a lot in some of the spaces that I'm deeply researching, whether it's biotechnology, software engineering, visual art, or sonic art, is a lot of conversation and speculation around the future. Some of this obsession with the future is related to this growing anxiety around industrial survival. I think of this growing interest in AI as connected to a collective anxiety, addressing all of this uncertainty by amassing large amounts of data and trying to create predictive models around ways we can "forecast" outcomes, or predict the future in certain ways. Something that I've been thinking about a lot is: how do we refuse the clamoring for certainty and practice wildness instead? How do we practice that uncertainty, that murkiness to build or to perform the worlds we need in the present moment?

NG

How does that show up in your practice currently?

AZC

The site that I'm most interested in for practicing wildness or uncertainty or intuition is the classroom. Inside learning contexts where we can all come into a physical space, or even a Zoom room, as learners with no determined outcome, but we all have some sort of inputs that we're going to throw into the pot with no attachment to the result. Or no already named output, because once it's named, it's no longer wild. Once it's named, it's already owned. The classroom has really been a place where I feel really free to practice improvisation, and practice abstraction, and practice opacity. All of these things give us room to hold uncertainty and hold our wildness in playful ways that don't feel as terrifying.

NG

I would love to hear more about your journey with Seeda School, as I have had my own journey with unschooling and grassroots spaces.

AZC

It definitely started with wanting to learn how to code and carrying that curiosity from MySpace to playing around on the family computer, all the way to college where I would self-select out of a lot of the college classes where coding was being offered. It wasn't until after school I joined a coding bootcamp and just really felt like "this is not the way I want to learn." I went through my own unlearning process too. Both the unlearning and healing that needed to happen after exposure to academic spaces, then the healing and unlearning that needed to happen after exposure to the post-college "career advancement" spaces where it was very rigid, very deadline focused, very competition based, very self-sacrificing. I wondered: "What would it look like to build a school that taught you the skills that we are using on the web every day, but also had this expansive political framework of Black feminism and this expansive philosophical framework of how we can also think about coding as fashioning, or building different modes, or ideas of being?"I had been teaching coding since 2018 but it wasn't until 2022 that I actually started teaching coding through a Black feminist lens and inviting learners into the space. Seeda School's name is inspired by seed data, Octavia Butler's *Earthseed* series, the seed shape of fractals, ancestors braiding seeds into our hair as a transportation technology. It's based on all these things. I wrote a book based in a parallel universe called Cykofa where Seeda is a non-binary biotechnologist character. I also wanted to name the school after this timeless ancestor that is simultaneously of the past, the future, and the present. We're learning inside those prompts.

NG

What I love about that, aside from the power of Black and diasporic lineages and legacy building from a place that's not empire, is how this school is itself a prototype. With my unschooling endeavors and grassroots projects, it feels like a prototype. It's not like, "I want this to be the biggest thing in the world and everyone needs to do this." It's like, "How can I go deep and imbue every detail of the construction of this space with meaning that makes new modes of relating possible?"

For the collective I was helping run called Radical Love Consciousness, our school was part of this program we called Re-Indigenizing Education. We defined indigenization as a twofold process. One, the decomposition of ideals and systems established in colonization. And two, a re-memory of ancient modes of connecting and knowledge, sharing knowledge, tending. To me, it sounds like you're also engaged in this process of trying to indigenize education by having this localized, broadened context. The world-building is happening at every level. That is the kind of depth and rigor that I find to be really unique and special to Black feminist praxis across the board.

The term intersectionality is thrown around like madness nowadays, but we come from a place where you can't just have one strand of a thing. It's a process of ideologies and disciplines and lenses. That's the world-building. It's the kaleidoscope that's formed from all of those different facets. I identify as a coder because I consider language to be coding. Interacting with people is coding because that builds the world.

AZC

Exactly! I would love to hear more about your framing of the clinic as a classroom, and how our healing practices and our healing journey are also places that teach us and help us unlearn. For me, the devotion came after I began healing. It awakened in me this conviction. It was through that healing journey that I said, "This is the only option." So I would love to hear more about your dreams about data and healing.

NG

Two quotes come to mind. One, in thinking about the trauma of academia, there's this Rumi quote that "the wound is where the light enters you." I think about that after being heartbroken by academia for a range of reasons, primarily racialized violence. That wound really is where this light entered me about thinking and about new structures out of necessity, the same necessity you're speaking of. And the second reference that came to mind is the quote by Toni Cade Bambara, that "our job is to make the revolution irresistible."

The Data Healing Recovery Clinic is a project I'm so excited to be tending to in a more focused capacity over the next year and a half with this fellowship that I'm doing at the Stanford Digital Civil Society Lab. Data healing is something that was born as this speculative project and convening body to talk about the psychosocial trauma of the internet that we experience. It's inspired by being introduced to the phrase "data trauma" by Olivia Ross, who is a really brilliant technologist and filmmaker.

The clinic is meant to take the form of a speculative workbook. It would have the kind of programmatic structure that a therapeutic clinic focused on addressing, healing, and recovering from psychosocial trauma would have, specifically one that is funded from reparations from these social media behemoths who make hundreds of billions of dollars, none of which make it back to the social media laborers that we've become. We sustain these platforms and their advertising models, and allow these platforms to be lucrative for a select few who are running them. There's a number of lawsuits that have been filed in the last couple years. Actually, when I got to Kenya in December, there had just been one that was filed for $1.6 billion. And it was a collection of organizations including Amnesty International who filed this lawsuit to the Kenyan high court suing Meta for the hate speech and ethnic violence that has been fueled on their platforms in the region.

I foresee more and more of those lawsuits not only being filed, but also being won. And once they are won, my hope is that some of those funds will be able to go towards these centers or these pop-up clinics. This workbook will give language to some of the somatic and psychological experiences that we face as a result of being online so much, while also innovating what healthier, more liberatory alternatives could look like and actually funding towards that innovation coming to life. We just need the space and the resources to make the other things, and it doesn't take over the world if your micro-community has a platform that has your shared values, your shared longings, your shared needs. That is enough.

Part of the damage of social media–giant culture is this idea that a platform is only meaningful or significant if it's being used by millions and billions of people. Re-indigenization, and Indigenous culture in general, has a different sense of scale. It really prioritizes intimacy, localization, and specificity over mass reach, which is a value system of empire that is outdated and that no longer serves us. Data Healing Recovery Clinic is going to be a network of pop-up and semi-permanent centers, spaces, and activations that take steps in this direction.

AZC

So much of this goes back to the interface of intuition, or distributed mutual aid, or care work as technologies. A vision that I've been tossing around inside Seeda School is what it would look like to refuse domination and expansion, and instead think about going deeper and think about mimicking a root network, so to speak, or even a forest floor more specifically. We have this network of public spaces here in the States of public libraries and public schools. What would it look like to leverage public libraries, and say, "Okay, we have this workbook and we have this free, open-source curriculum." What would it look like to make that available to folks? If there's a practitioner in Detroit, for example, who wants to take this curriculum and have a pop-up school in their public library or pop-up classroom in their public library? How can we work in these distributed ways of cooperativism?

So much of this hardware that we are surrounding ourselves with and that we're connected by is actually inspired by the ways a forest or an ecosystem works. How can the forest floor, or the ecosystem of the forest, actually inspire a way of working or a way of playing with knowledge and sharing knowledge? I have this dream of there being networks of pop-up classrooms in public libraries leveraging the micro-moments that are already, like you said, happening in local communities. Moving forward, whether it's intuition or mutual aid, they have been our teachers.

NG

I remember in 2021, I was on this whole wave. I was like, "How do we make love go viral?" All these other things are going viral. How do we make love go viral? And I reached this epiphany: it doesn't need to go viral. It needs to go fractal. What you're describing is exactly that, mimicking this patterning of the forest floor of these root systems and having these frameworks spread in that way. It's inherently emergent and it inherently reaches more people and gets more nutrients to them the same way that mycorrhizal networks do. I've been thinking a lot about it in the Kenyan context where we don't necessarily have a public library system throughout the country that is robust, which necessitates more of the pop-up from the ground up type vibe.

I was just writing in my little data healing journal that I want to use this fellowship to buy 100 children's books that deal with different political leaders and freedom fighters from the country and distribute them in rural areas and have people come together and essentially have these be spaces where people get to be offline and online at the same time. That's what the library is, right? There's the computer access, but there are the books. The library is the mother tree.

Even this dialogue with you feels like a microcosm of what is possible and what is begging to be experienced in connection. Here, we're building constellations together and the lights that I'm working with are talking to yours and together they make a map.

SAM LAVIGNE & OR ZUBLASKY

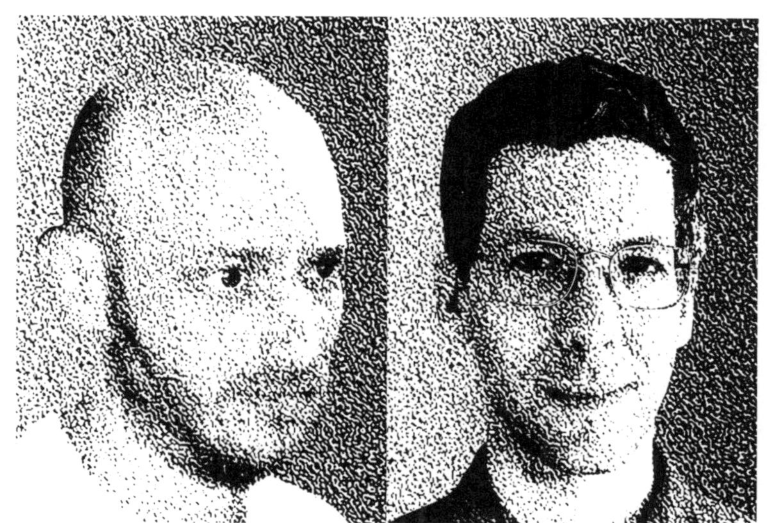

On What Artists Can Bring to Movement Spaces

Artists and educators Sam Lavigne and Or Zubalsky in conversation about the limitations of art within organizing and the possibilities of leveraging the tools we have access to in order to mobilize together.

This conversation between Sam Lavigne and Or Zubalsky happened over Zoom in March of 2023. It has been edited for length and clarity.

Or Zubalsky

I participated in the strike last year at The New School, as an adjunct, and it was really interesting to see how organizing across different parts of the community within this university happened through digital organizing structures. I've never seen anything like it in terms of the speed and scale, while also being private. I think it's related to Covid in many ways. Before the pandemic, my experience of people coming together to organize and mobilize was in person, even in very large groups. With this, it felt like people were very practiced in communicating remotely, even in huge groups. At The New School, a WhatsApp group of part-time faculty just emerged and grew very, very quickly to have hundreds of people. A lot of other groups emerged based on different overlaps that people had.

Sam Lavigne

I love that that kind of organizing work needs to happen, in a sense, in public anyway, without the expectation that you're going to be able to surprise the people that you're organizing in opposition to. Do you think it mattered that there might have been administrators in those WhatsApp groups?

OZ

I think it depends on the nature of the action that's being planned. For picketing outside of a university building, it's orchestrated and understood on all of the sides. With direct action, the element of surprise can be strategic.

SL

As someone working within the intersections of politics, technology, and art-making, I wonder about your general feeling about the role that these tools can play. Do you have an optimistic or a pessimistic disposition to them, or feel that we should use whatever is at our disposal at the time and it's nothing more or less than that?

OZ

I would say that I'm optimistic, but it's not exclusive to digital technology. The tools are available. They're being manipulated really effectively by other actors, like right-wing and fascist factions, who are using digital technology and leveraging the affordances that these digital systems have. It feels like it's working for them and that maybe progressive movements are a little behind.

SL

My suspicion is that most of the tools have some kind of regressive or reactionary essence to them. I'm not saying that there's an essential quality they have that's reactionary or conservative, but maybe it's more that they're emerging from reactionary and conservative contexts and therefore it's somehow a little bit easier for them to be deployed towards those ends. That would be a hypothesis, but not something I feel strong confidence in.

OZ

In terms of popular tools and popular systems, they're already designed within a super capitalist mindset. The value systems that are built into the tools are not radical to begin with, nor reflective, nor critical.

I was thinking about how scraping, which is a big part of your practice, is so effective because digital technology doesn't have to be using an existing system and trying to work within it. It can also be just doing the kind of research that needs to be done to gather resources in order to work more effectively. I haven't heard scraping brought up so often in the kind of organizing spaces that I've been to.

SL

I think people are starting to clue into it a little bit, but it's probably something that still feels weird. There's not a kind of built-in imagination for how you could make use of it. People also use words like "open-source intelligence" to talk about the scraping approach. For me, it's really obvious that there's an edge that could be had by leveraging what is freely available on the open web, or perhaps what you might have to pay a little bit of money for but is still not expensive.

Organizers should always be thinking about whatever tools they have at their disposal. I'm thinking of Sean Black, an activist who used web automation tools to send fake job applications to the Kellogg's company website when they were trying to hire during a strike. You have an automatic form fill-out project too. Could you share a little bit about that project?

OZ

That project was done at a moment when the Israeli state archive was being digitized. I went there to do research at the physical archive, but I saw that none of the records were available to the general public. Instead, the records would only be available through the digital interface but the archive had just begun the process and most of the records had not been digitized yet. They had their own queue and their own set of priorities of what material to make public and when. However, they did have an online form interface where, if you found a record that hadn't been digitized yet, you could request it. Then, if the state deemed that the record can be made public, an archivist would scan the record and make it public and it would move to the front of the line. I found about 1,000 records, a collection of letters and requests that were made to the newly formed state of Israel in 1948 and 1949. Those requests were made by people who lived there before Israel became a state, mostly Palestinians. They were asking for access to their property, or permission to start a newspaper in Arabic. So I compiled my own set of records that I was interested in making public and then automated the process of filling out that form to request them. They did become public, it did work, but this sort of work doesn't address the urgency of the ongoing Nakba. A week ago, settlers set the Palestinian village Huwara on fire. In terms of effectiveness of actions like this, the project created more questions.

SL

In a way, on its own very limited terms that the project sets out for itself, it's a success. It's a technical, political, bureaucratic process that you're engaging with and it succeeds at that level, but then it fails in terms of a broader, more significant political action. Is that fair to say?

OZ

Yes. Also, the parameters of what is recorded in the first place are set by this national project.

Even if something is made public, it still speaks the language of the state. The archive as a whole still represents this effort of forming the collective identity or collective memory of that place from a Zionist nationalist perspective. That's also an issue. Individual letters that were made public do have value, but after working on this project I did feel more interested in taking action that is actually coming out of a collective conversation. How do we use these tactics in a way that supports the goals of a movement or a group of organizers rather than just a solo practice?

SL

It acts in isolation, a project like that. When I do these little interventions in my own work, I think about what their limitations are and try to be really open-eyed about the limitations of this type of approach. With these small-scale, solo interventions, there's a real limitation to them. They've become less about attempting to enact some kind of change and more about flushing something through the bureaucratic system that they're dealing with and trying to understand that system a little bit better, both in a technical sense, but also maybe a poetic sense as well.

OZ

Something that I really appreciate about your work is that, sometimes, the intervention appears to be one thing, but it is also operating on the structure of how the work circulates and is a part of different transactions. I'm thinking about *Fragile States*, where there is value to the material that's being produced, but also there is literal value that is exchanged. The work also intervenes in how funding works and takes an approach to re-granting. The intervention happens on multiple levels.

SL

This is a piece that emerged out of two other previous works, all of which are collaborations with Tega Brain. We'd been playing around with this notion of "expanded geoengineering." We were doing a series of projects that look at the relationship between data and ecology. The previous projects were *Synthetic Messenger*, which was about making a botnet to try to inflate the value of climate news, and then *Perfect Sleep*, which was about relationships between rest, sleep, and climate change. We, or at least I, had been feeling sort of increasingly insulated in these works that were about this existential threat and wanted to try to converse with activists who had been involved for a lot longer than either of us had. We had this opportunity from New York University who gave us a small-ish grant to do a "climate change" project.

These funny situations where a funding organization wants some project about X or Y or Z, and we had this idea that it would be good to find a way to channel funding from NYU to people who really needed it and who had also faced real, unfair consequences for their activism. I created an LLC called Redistribute LLC, and the LLC received that grant from NYU. Then we were able to pay directly to these climate activists, all of whom had been incarcerated for their activism.

This is intended to be an ongoing project. At the moment, we have four people that we've talked with. We do about an hour long interview with them, we transcribe the interview, and then we give them a stipend of $1,000 each. They get the stipend no matter what, even if they don't actually do the interview. We're not journalists, so we don't have to hold ourselves to a journalist's standards. We give them the full transcript afterwards, and they're able to make any edits that they want to. It's a set of interviews, but it's really guided and controlled by the interviewees. The people we talked to are Max Curmi, who was in Blockade Australia, and he shut down a port; Red Fawn Fallis, who was in Standing Rock and got four years for having a gun planted on her; "Rose," an activist from Extinction Rebellion Sudan, who really didn't do much more than pass out flyers but faced some really brutal consequences; and Daniel McGowan, who was a member of the Earth Liberation Front and spent seven years in jail for doing direct action. The exciting thing for us as we were thinking about how to make this was to think about who institutions like NYU support. What does it mean to make an "artwork" about climate change in 2022 or 2023? What does it look like when you're thinking how an academic timeline, or the timeline of producing something, might actually be longer than the time that we actually have to respond to the climate crisis? The project is responding to all of those questions, and hopefully also acting in its own way as direct action.

OZ

It has material effects that are so tangible. It's not about big data, nor reverse engineering some data structure, nor the algorithm that determines what gets viewed or shared. It's about the funding structures and grant logic, and that has so much power in how a technology shapes culture.

SL

It also creates an archive of direct eco-activism approaches too. So it has this dual purpose in that sense. Have you heard about this book, *A Miracle, A Universe*? It's about torture in Brazil and, specifically, the production of this archive that was made to help hold the previous regime to account. Basically, the Brazilian dictatorship was starting to collapse a bit, and on their way out they opened up the military archives that were containing records of military tribunals. It was this brief moment, and a group of activists decided to try to get all of the material from those archives. They did something that was ingenious. They were only allowed to take out one case at a time, so they would go in, request a case record, and then they would photocopy it and then they would return the original files. And in these military accounts there were a lot of incidents of people confessing. There was also a lot of people, during these accounts, who would also describe what had happened to them in jail, which included torture. It became a series of records of the crimes of the regime. What's amazing about it is how the records were taken out of the archive. The activists rented an office and bought a bunch of copying machines, creating an assembly line of taking records out, photocopying them, shipping the photocopies out of the country, and then returning the records. This process is something that I am extremely interested in. It was a procedure for duplicating an archive. There's something incredibly inspiring about that. An independent record collecting and archiving in the face of adversity, I suppose, as a political project.

OZ

It being in a physical media feels so important in terms of the safety of these records. Creating an archive from an archive is a form of resistance that then can be augmented or be given new dimensions and new context.

SL

There's a theme in your work around absence of records. Can you speak to how absence plays a role for you?

OZ

It's definitely a theme. I'm interested in this condition of not knowing something that is actually unknowable or unspeakable, especially as it relates to collective trauma. For me, it shows up in the absence and the gaps that exist in the material that is produced by a settler colonialist project like Israel. It comes up in looking at the state archive, but it comes up also in looking at how history is taught.

Growing up in Israel was, in many ways, based on the Palestinian catastrophe being rendered invisible. Then, as somebody whose grandparents are Holocaust survivors, there's another relationship to collective trauma that is very well recorded but also unreachable in many ways. I'm trying to grapple and understand and relate to these limitations, especially as experiences are translated to text and to metadata and all these forms that are just lacking in so many ways. I'm finding recently that software and the structure of code are ways to access this kind of complexity. This is what *Merge Conflicts* is doing. It's a series of tutorials that tries to teach how to use Git, a system for version control and managing multiple versions of digital documents and their time-lines and changes, and uses manipulated history textbooks from Israel as the material that is being recorded. The recording history command in Git is such an explicit process. Every moment has to be decided in such a clear way, "This is something I want to record, and this is something that's important to save as a moment that can be returned to," versus this history curriculum that has its own implicit way of recording history. I'm finding that software as a structure helps me understand this relationship to not knowing because it makes things so explicit.

SL

Git is software that's built with a very particular purpose in mind, which is, as you say, to produce recoverable landmarks or something. So you're making a history for other people to look at so that they can ideally make sense of how code went from one place to another place. I think that, of course, history textbooks, particularly history textbooks for children, are also built with a particular purpose in mind. It's a wonderful way to use software as a metaphor that becomes this really nice way of looking at history texts.

OZ

I'm just trying to find a balance between making work as an individual and working within all of these other political contexts that are more collective. It's really a big challenge. I don't have any resolution, but I am interested in what artists with these specific fluencies in software and in tactical media can bring to movement spaces and to political organizing, and the kind of trust that is necessary in order for these contributions to be made. What does that look like, and what kind of technology will support building that sort of trust?

SL

In an art context, everything is set up to reward an interiority, an individualism. On the other hand, there are real technical needs that activists have, and that people who experiment with technology really can start to fill, potentially. The danger, of course, always is risk. For example, I would never want to be in charge of making a robust communication platform for an activist organization or group of activists because the risk is so high. If you mess it up, then the consequences are potentially really high. With some of these works, is producing a technical spectacle something that's interesting in a political space or is it something that should be avoided? It's very easy to create spectacle using technology. What's more difficult is to think about ways that could be strategically beneficial.

OZ

I completely agree. There was a moment during the strike at The New School where students and full-time faculty started to organize as well, but they didn't really have—especially the full-time faculty—a way to communicate with each other at the necessary scale because the leadership of the university is the only body that has access to broadcast a message to The New School community. It became clear that it would be useful to be able to communicate to the entire faculty body. The directory of faculty is available online and someone could very easily scrape that directory and get all of the addresses to shift how communication can take place. The only thing that it took in order for that to happen was for someone to be involved and be plugged into the conversation of the needs that were surfacing and to respond to it with these sort of skills.

It's really nice to see how there's a range of needs that come up in the process of organizing. These needs can be met with different sorts of skill sets and experiences. It feels like this fluency with data structures, software, and patterns of web design are useful. They can contribute and meet certain needs. It's important to be there, to be plugged in, and to be able to respond or to be able to have a friend who can respond.

When I say that I wonder what kind of technology can support building trust and taking action collectively, maybe the technology is just making dinner together.

EILEEN ISAGON SKYERS & DOROTHY SANTOS

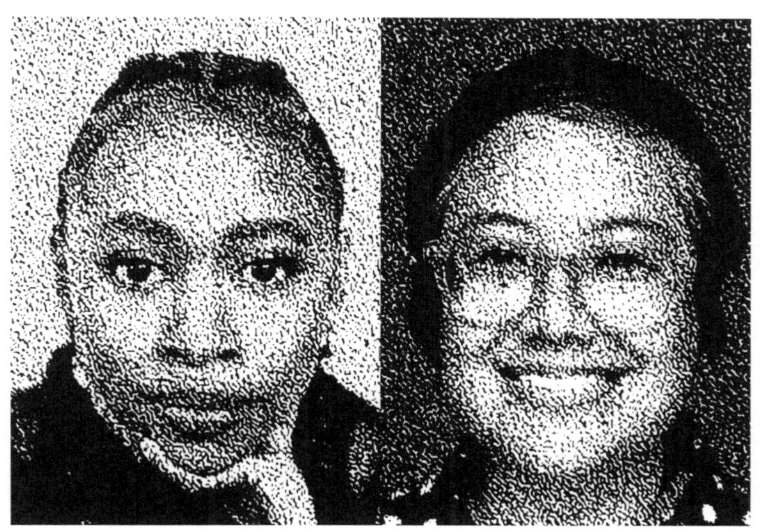

On Open-Source Software as Ideology

Curator Eileen Isagon Skyers talks with writer, artist, and educator Dorothy Santos about open-source software, pre-colonial mythology, and the nexus of technology and affect.

This conversation between Eileen Isagon Skyers and Dorothy Santos happened over Zoom in March of 2023. It has been edited for length and clarity.

Eileen Isagon Skyers

Let's begin by talking about your relationship to open-source software as an ideology, political framework and form of dialogue. How can open-source software be a global peripatetic network or pedagogy in its own right?

Dorothy Santos

Open-source software as a modality or methodology for people to learn how to code and build ecosystems is what drew me to it initially. I did experiment with Processing many years ago, before I went to California College of the Arts to pursue my master's degree. I originally wanted to be an artist who did illustration and design but quickly realized that wasn't for me, so I began coding in a very novice way, inspired by artists who were playing with code as poetry.

During an artist residency at Banff in Canada, I took a workshop with Lillian-Yvonne Bertram, the author of *Travesty Generator*. That's when I found the programming language I needed to work in thereafter. Bertram's framing around coding was so similar to the way I looked at it. QTBIPOC, disabled, immigrant folks in the open-source community actually opened me up to many new possibilities because they constantly have to think creatively. Artists were getting creative with this technology and subverting it.

EIS

There is so much obfuscating language around these opaque frameworks that contribute to the theatrics of technology. I know this, in part, because I've worked on UX copy for developers and startups. I'm curious what kind of systems you think we ought to replicate with technology. Working within and against these spaces, whose utopias are being built here? And by whom?

DS

I was actually talking to a good friend, Dr. Gabi Schaffzin, about what it means to construct systems and processes in the material world that are *actually needed* versus things that are nice to have. What might it look like if we actually borrowed from systems we learned growing up, or from platforms we've used that served a very specific function, and ran with those ideas?

At the height of the pandemic, for instance, mutual aid was very central. It came to the fore, suddenly, as a way to take care of one another. And Indigenous communities—Black, brown, Latinx, disabled community members—had already been doing that. I look at Filipino culture, and I think about that type of configuration…

EIS

Hospitality, shared resources…

DS

Exactly. When I imagine what it feels like to work with technology you haven't worked with, I consider the friendly error system of the p5 community. You can make an error, and the system doesn't reprimand you for making a mistake. When I've presented my own creative practice (often to a predominantly cis straight white audience), pretty scathing things have been said about my work. Like: "Well, how does that explore prosody? So many people have already done voice recognition work. How is this adding to that?" I am making art. I'm not making a product. So if I'm replicating anything, it's because I'm using the existing technology as a prompt for what's *not* working. I want to see more protective technologies that stem from frames of mutual aid and the kinds of care that we saw growing up.

EIS

I love that you spoke about the abstract language embedded in technology. The attitude of a 404 error, for instance, is so loaded. It is not neutral. But it's something that we have taken for granted as part of our day-to-day reality. As we move toward the next evolution of the internet—toward concepts like the metaverse, and toward a more embodied internet—what are some lessons that can be learned from the earlier web's open-source ethos?

DS

The first lesson that comes to my mind is that not everything has to be a product. Not everything has to be sold. I wish that playfulness was a thing. I'm not even necessarily talking about joy. I have a tendency in my own creative practice to make games, but the games are not necessarily fun. They're often very emotionally charged, and they offer a ludic experience. There is still an incentive to get to the end, or to finish, but it is through difficult tasks that someone can cease to do when they choose. And that's kind of the point. It's very synonymous with life.

How do we engage in play, but also: how do we avoid the compulsion to make something to sell that commodifies yet another string of data or information? When there's a technical mishap, my partner, artist and scholar Abram Stern, jokingly always says, "Computers were a mistake." I say something a little different. I say, "Social media was a mistake." It tells you what you *think* you want to hear, depending on how you navigate. Talk about an embodied experience. A lot of our activity online is described as navigation—as something very physical, like "surfing." I'm reminded of Mendi and Keith Obadike, and their work *Blackness for Sale*. When Keith talks about that work, he talks about a very colonialist semantic. There's Amazon, there's eBay... How do we bring back respect and honor for material reality that isn't used for commercial, capitalist, or colonialist gain in the digital space?

EIS

This touches on how earlier forms of the web may have had a different teleology. Because it was early, there was that unknowing, and there was more room to engage in play, and sometimes even breakage. Glitch wasn't necessarily seen as negative. I want to talk, of course, about *Cyborg's Prosody*, your digital project that I understand as a mobile application and artistic intervention.

DS

Much of my research is focused on voice recognition, speech technologies, and assistive tech. I study and research how human voices are trained. There are synthetic voices and voice cloning, and I often think about telephone operators and 911 dispatchers as this conception of the human body. Those occupations are perceived as programmable. Anna Friz, one of my mentors at University of California, Santa Cruz, has actually reminded me that the human body is a recording device because it has its own memory; it has its own hardware. We do have our own hardware to consider. I thought about that deeply when I was researching accent reduction schools, which are very common. So, *Cyborg's Prosody* is a satirical work in response to these accent induction schools. There are many language learning apps like Rosetta Stone, Duolingo, Babbel, or Memrise, however, you're not necessarily learning the affect and embodiment of the language itself.

EIS

You're not learning emphasis and emotion.

DS

Exactly. When you greet someone, you say *kumusta ka na*, there's intonation, there's prosody. So I created an accent *induction* school. The project became very personal. Initially, I based it on what Filipino call center workers were learning. They are required to take American cultural competency classes, which is strange because they are learning American stereotypes—which is its own conundrum. But *Cyborg's Prosody* became a game about my mother and her grappling with her mother tongue.

The game levels are based on Elizabeth Kubler Ross's five stages of grief, and each of those levels are vignettes. Each vignette is about 500 to 800 words, and they stem from these intense conversations where I interviewed my mom about each stage of grief. Each question was based on her experience learning

English the "American" way. It's compulsory to learn English in the Philippines, but learning American English is very different.

The vignettes are based on how her anger showed up, how denial showed up, how she bargained her way through language. It's filled with stories of loss and displacement—of the semantic, migratory path. In the game, you're prompted to repeat the bolded text, and you can only progress if you successfully repeat the cyborg. The cyborg I'm using has my mom's voice.

The project decenters whiteness, Americanness, Westernness and Britishness, because those are the defaults. I'm using aspects of technology as a way of pointing out what's wrong with it. And showing why it's important to think about accent bias, and the technologies that aim to eliminate accents. I use "the colonization of voice" in my dissertation title because I believe that's what this software is often doing. It tries to course correct or discipline your body so that you literally can't speak to who you are.

EIS

There is an assumption that making someone sound more American or Western would improve their mental health because that is inherently "good" or "better" or more productive for them in life. You've reminded me of a project by Eva and Franco Mattes called *Dark Content* (2015). It centers conversations with internet content moderators, many of whom are paid incredibly low wages. As you know, the Philippines employs a high concentration of content moderators. Eva and Franco used a vocal manipulator to anonymize the workers. It's as if people are acting as the algorithm, but those very people are not even recognized as core contributors to this kind of work. There's always an assumption that Black and brown work, queer work, and feminist work has not critically contributed to our technology.

DS

There is a twisted, complicated history of content moderation and call center work respectively. There's a literature scholar who teaches at Rice University, Alden Sajor Marte-Wood, who writes about Filipino care work as it relates to technology. There was a content moderator in the Philippines who said that she feels that it's her duty because she's called upon by God to do this work. And in my mind I'm like, "No–that's not your responsibility." With 911 operating and dispatching, those workers are not necessarily trained on things like cultural competency, cultural sensitivity, or accent bias. New technologies are being explored to assist with detecting language. A lot of dispatchers suffer from PTSD, carpal tunnel, or repetitive stress injury.

EIS

They are in extremely high-stress situations for long periods of time.

DS

A dispatcher's adrenaline levels are heightened for their entire shift because they have to treat every call as an emergency. My understanding and delving into these ecosystems of how communication and telecommunications work has illuminated how technology touches all parts of our lives.

EIS

And then what does it mean when those systems are biased, or working in favor of some and against others? I'm drawn to this story of the moderator that felt she was called upon by a higher power to do this work. I have been thinking about precolonial mythology in the Philippines, and researching Indigenous Filipino practices that were lost to Western theology. Tracing the digital circuit as far back as early divination, I'm curious whether you feel like animism can be recast within the computational, or rational, side.

DS

There is often a misunderstanding that you don't have to understand how technology works–that there is a mysticism, or magic, behind it. But there's not; that's not what magic is about. I myself have been delving into Indigenous Filipino cultures and deities in recent years. My parents immigrated here, so they didn't want me to grow up as a Filipino kid. They wanted me to grow up as an American. I was raised to be American, not knowing the cognitive, emotional, intellectual repercussions of this disavowal. I have relied on my own curiosity and related to younger generations who are Filipino American, American-born, or children of the diaspora, such as yourself, who are reconnecting and honoring these sides of ourselves that we were told *ought not be*. A lot of that comes through my tarot practice, but it also comes through language. I'm teaching myself Tagalog. It is wild to think about the multiplicity of language and semantics and the embeddedness of meaning and subtext in my own speech. Learning language as an adult fascinates me. I feel that it's a form of incantation. That's why I take language so seriously. There are certain things in the Tagalog language that—returning to your question about animism and returning to mythologies—have no clear-cut definition.

EIS

There are words that cannot be translated.

DS

Yes, like *kapwa*.

EIS

Right. *Pakikipagkapwa* has this meaning akin to our relationship to the earth, plants, animals, and to all other beings. There's no word for that in English.

DS

Something that I have fought to resist is the attempt to directly translate every language into something I know. Sometimes it's not about that; it's about listening carefully and understanding that even language has its own sacredness.

EIS

You also speak another language, which is code. I've thought a lot about code language, metaphorically, as a form of alchemy—as this series of signs and symbols that can transmogrify and attain objecthood through technology. If we are reaching this nexus of technology and affect within these massive coded ecosystems, I'm curious how you approach code language with care or sensitivity to different kinds of human transmission.

DS

I'm glad you brought that up because I recently contributed to something called *The Critical Coding Cookbook*, a publication by Xin Xin and Katherine Moriwaki. I called my exercise *Ways of Being*. It was inspired by a conversation I facilitated during my fellowship at Yerba Buena Center for the Arts. It included Lauren Lee McCarthy, Elizabeth Travelslight, Adrian Jones, Joanne Rondilla, and Xiaowei Wang. And the exercise involved taking your favorite line of code and remixing it into a poem, or prose. What we know as punctuation often becomes part of the syntax in code. I've done this exercise myself. For example, my favorite line of code is "console.log()." Console log and the parentheses. The console.log() outputs the message you are trying to deliver to the web console. While that sounds basic to some people, it is one of my favorite commands. Another example: if you use forward slash in your code, it's like a whisper. It's behind the scenes. The code doesn't actually appear.

There are different configurations of punctuation that serve as pathways, or prompts, for the coder on the backend. I realize that while I'm learning code, I'm also engaging in poeticism. The more code I try to learn, the more poetic I am trying to be. Code can be re-introduced as a prompt to be creative–to upend, or subvert, what exists. And that's why I believe in open-source software. I have hope in it because there are different creators–people coming from different languages and backgrounds–who approach this technology from entirely different perspectives. People forget that we can make magic through technology.

The title of this interview reference's Wendy Hui Kyong Chun's "On Software or the Persistence of Visual Knowledge."

MANUEL ARTURO ABREU

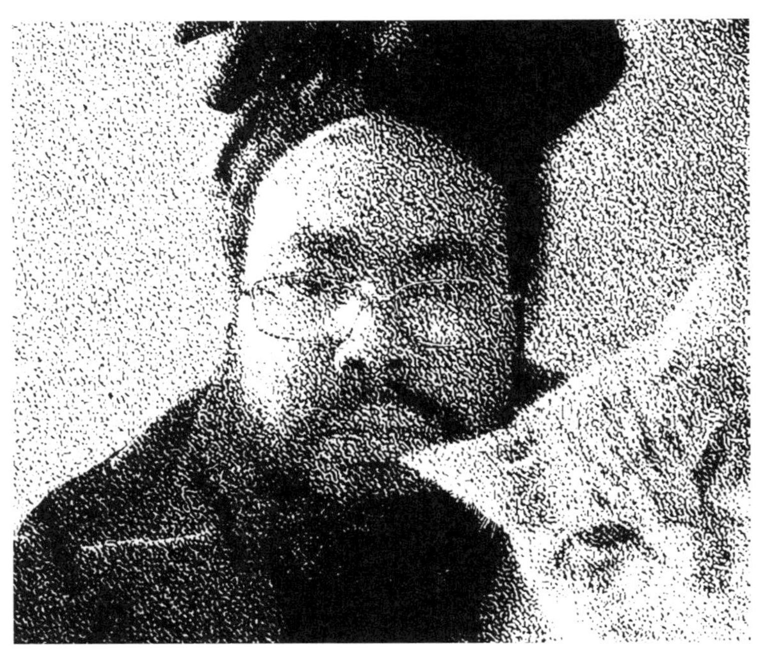

On Caribbean Mythopoetic Pedagogies.

home school is a free pop-up art school and space of sacred duty co-founded by Victoria Anne Reis and me in 2015. When Victoria returned to Oregon, she was no longer able to participate in the local offerings of BHQFU (then an unaccredited, free collaborative program based in Brooklyn). As someone interested in distance learning, I suggested we start our own alternative arts education project. We wanted to take a genre-non-conforming approach, creating welcoming spaces for critical engagement with contemporary art with a focus on remote participants, live-streamed and archived on YouTube and Tumblr. We've programmed artist talks, classes, poetry readings, field days, performances, publications, exhibitions, and more.

Recently, I have developed and executed six online courses, called Alt Hist Abs, pursuing an alternative history of abstraction. My project examines functional, socially and spiritually embedded abstraction, re-situating the Western origin myth of abstraction as a functionless, autotelic objet d'art that presents just one version of the story. I also develop courses that cover pivotal thinkers of the Afro-Caribbean philosophical and mythopoetic traditions, including Sylvia Wynter (A New Science of the Word) and Wilson Harris (Quantum Fiction). I examine the dynamics of what Wilson Harris calls "omens of capacity" in the colonial encounter in courses such as ZOMBIE: Fear of a Black Republic and Carib, Caliban, Cannibal: the Columbian encounter and resistant forms-of-life.

In the genealogy of abstraction put forth by this project, socially embedded art is positioned in contrast to the European conception of the objet d'art. Mathematician Ron Eglash traces the digital circuit back to West African divination, but his analysis lacks a proper understanding of the coloniality of this development–in particular, the devaluation of African people and African social and spiritual technologies which form the basis of Western computation once stripped of their Africanness, religiosity, and context. My practice (including both my moving-image works and the courses that I teach) humbly attempts to distill into an area of focus the contemporary strategies for "re-enchanting" the aesthetic–the computational, and the rational, which, following Eglash, are but footnotes to African divination and fractal structural systems.

I would love to situate the Alt Hist Abs endeavor within home school. I spend a lot of time with myself, and with my co-director Victoria Anne Reis, discussing this gray area. home school projects are free and public. On the other hand, I offer my Alt Hist Abs curriculum at a sliding scale, with an open enrollment process and, in certain cases, pricier one-on-one tutoring. Both home school and Alt Hist Abs dovetail with respect to critical and space-making aims, leaning heavily on digital circulation and gathering. Indeed, home school's primary aim since it began in 2015 has been to further distance learning through live streaming and digital archives.

While the project of home school has changed a lot along the way, we remain committed to producing high-quality edutainment around contemporary art and its issues. We have also been reframing the project as a space of sacred duty. Our residency at Oregon Contemporary for their eleventh curator-in-residence season involves three exhibitions and accompanying programming that address the following questions: How can art communities behave in sacred duty to one another and to the world at large? In what ways can and should art spaces become spaces of sacred community? In what sense is the concept of "art" itself, having originated from European Christian theology, spiritually bereft or repressing some deep mystery? Our curatorial efforts at Oregon Contemporary have been informed by our commitment to shared embodied experience after five years of distance learning–oriented curriculum, reflection on mortality, and community responsibility.

My interests within my own artistic practice have been situated in ephemeral sculpture, the transformation of found material, and sculptural thinking in general as a critical mode of engaging materiality, space, and context. However, for a period, the pandemic stymied the sculptural component of my practice. It also signaled a shift toward a vernacular moving-image pedagogy leveraging digital circulation (via YouTube, Instagram, etc.). As I reflect back, I realize that I've been applying sculptural thinking to the production of these video works, curricula, and other material.

My vernacular moving image pedagogy practice began when Los Angeles–based artist and philosopher Mandy Harris Williams commissioned *qué significa ser latinx* (2019)[1] for an Ace Hotel Latinx History Month event. This video critiqued the eugenic concept of mestizaje and the contemporary youth rejection of Latinidad. I stitched together found videos on the topic with my own commentary. I produced this work while in residence at Centrum at Fort Worden, Port Townsend, Washington. Spotty internet necessitated its lo-fi aesthetic.

Video proved to be useful as a critical space, especially when applying the sculptural techniques of incorporating, arranging, juxtaposing, and commenting on found material. Its ephemerality is like an emergent property: it arrives at the moment of cognition of the network of materials, all their resonances and dissonances. I continued working in this mode with a video work called *An Alternative History of Abstraction* (2020),[2] which rejects the European modernist origin myth of abstraction and the functionless, autonomous art object in favor of an older Black and brown lineage of functional, socially and spiritually embedded, non-autonomous abstraction. In the work, I discuss Tang-era calligraphy,

1. https://www.youtube.com/watch?v=dnt2TYEMSGs

2. https://www.youtube.com/watch?v=A8CeRo3lQQQ

3. https://www.wmagazine.com/story/cassandra-press-redefines-the-way-black-critical-theory-is-taught

wildstyle graffiti, the Gee's Bend quilters, and J.B. Murray and James Hampton's Black religious asemic writing, to name a few. The piece was commissioned by Discrit and debuted online with Atlanta Contemporary. There was an implicit link in my mind between somewhat opaque and ephemeral sculptural gestures and historical processes of ornamentation of the textual toward illegibility (such as in calligraphy).

I realized that the kind of social/study experience of producing and sharing this work with the public—and the work's functionality insofar as its pedagogical and critical nature—directly mirrored the functional, embedded character of the type of abstract aesthetic labor I analyzed in the video. Los Angeles-based artist Kandis Williams also noted that there was room to delve deeper into both the violence of "abstraction" as the secularized vestige of Christian rejection of the sinful material world, and the Black weaponization of abstraction against this colonial order of knowing. She astutely shares in an interview with *W* magazine: "the first [type of abstraction] is modern abstraction, born out of the colonial European encounter with the indigenous. The second is Black abstraction, the African-based conceptual thought (like carving an ancestor into a glyph on a rock and praying to it, or creating a family pattern to be woven for generations), and the third is Black Marxist abstraction."[3]

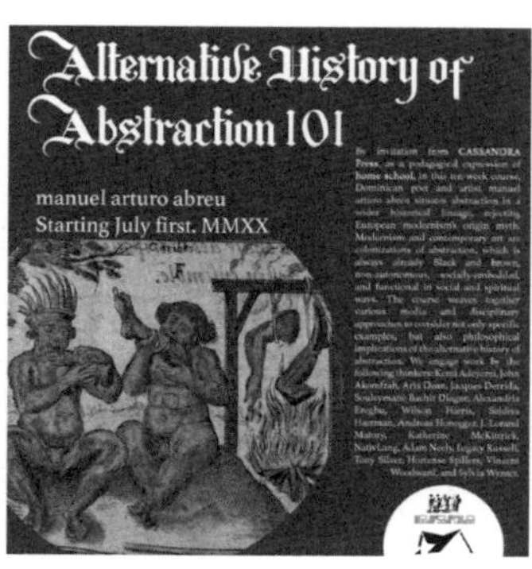

Alternative History of Abstraction 101 class poster designed by abreu, June 2020.

At Williams's invitation, I expanded the ideas from the Alternative History of Abstraction into a ten-week course of the same name, offered in July 2020 via CASSANDRA Press,[4] an artist-run publishing and educational platform founded by Williams, which produces lo-fi printed matter, classes, projects, artist books, and exhibitions. Executing a project of this scope showed me the pedagogical potential of semi-publicly demonstrating my independent research interests in the vernacular moving-image format. A network of juxtaposed sources creates a kind of choreography of study; exploring its social components allows for the development of critical perspectives. The development of new concepts to parse the network of assigned material promises greater sensory granularity, and the particular sociality of struggling with meaning resonates with the overall frame of rejecting the Euro-colonization of abstraction.

This is of interest to me because video, as a medium, has the unique power to discipline the public into the Western consumer mindset. It is an equivocal medium—one that becomes explosive with broader circulation. Its radical potential can (and must) challenge its normative antiblack disciplinary role. The circulation of moving images documenting the humiliation, maiming, and murder of Black people is the contemporary Silicon version of lynching mementos (a choice mode of entertainment for nineteenth-century white Americans who may have missed the live event). As Aria Dean argues: "the history of black people in the Americas…is intrinsically bound up with the history of mass media and photographic and moving images."[5]

I created another moving image work in the vein of vernacular pedagogy while teaching the Alternative History of Abstraction 101 course. *Debajo del agua: the wake work of Enerolisa Núñez* (2020)[6] centers

4. https://www.cassandra-press.org/classrooms

5. Aria Dean, "On the black generic," National Gallery of Victoria, 2017, https://www.ngv.vic.gov.au/exhibition_post/on-the-black-generic.

6. https://youtu.be/pghmUTfgyjg

Dominican musician and spiritual-cultural worker Enerolisa Núñez and her salve criolla music. Here, I analyze the concept of folklore/roots as a site of capture and deracialization of Núñez's spiritual labor and aesthetics in the context of Dominican antiblackness and tourist-modernity. More recently, I've been teaching a class called ZOMBIE: Fear of a Black Republic, which analyzes the origin of the "zombie" trope during the US occupation of Haiti (1915–34) and its continuity with European fears of a Black rebel contagion in the wake of the Haitian Revolution (1791–1804). Moving forward, the Alternative History of Abstraction will continue to draw from two simultaneous impulses: general critical work, and region- or maker-specific work.

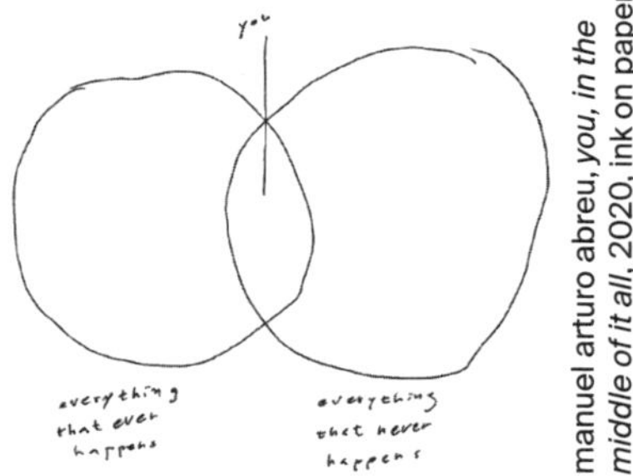

manuel arturo abreu, *you, in the middle of it all*, 2020, ink on paper.

I received the Support Beam grant from the Regional Arts and Culture Council in Oregon (RACC) to continue this line of work. For this grant, I am working on a new series of videos about artists based in the Pacific Northwest. I'll be making videos about Thelma Johnson Streat, sharita towne, damali ayo, Noah Davis, Natalie Ball, and others. I'm inspired by the concept of placemaking as explored by makers and thinkers from the region who are dealing with contemporary manifestations of colonialism and antiblackness while rejecting a static, vestigial concept of "tradition." I think it would be fitting to make a video about myself as well (given that my public practice started in the wake of my arrest). The Northwest has a special relationship to craft that deserves exploration in the context of Indigenous abstraction, its long history, and its survivance. Whether specific considerations about video as a medium or sculptural thinking in relation to video will find its way into this body of work remains to be seen, but I am excited to be making this work and grateful for this support from RACC's Support Beam. I hope that, in some small way, this body of work can operate as a form of speculative placemaking and be of service to the aesthetic history and future of the Pacific Northwest region.

Student input

Sam Osaro
Reed College: Making Space 09/21/22

Last fall, I accompanied my dear friend and teacher manuel arturo abreu to their alma mater, Reed College, to gather with a group of fellow students for a class called Making Space.

The days leading up to our gathering were spent reflecting on my experience in manuel's seminal course ZOMBIE: Fear of a Black Republic. I felt strongly that I wanted to "sum up" the coursework, along with my experience of it. Within a few minutes of replaying our old conversations, I was convinced that this was not at all possible. I decided against trying to caption the universe, and out came a testimony of sorts. What follows is what I read aloud at Reed College on September 21st, 2022, to capture that experience:

In preparation for our gathering today, and my student testimony, I return to the final discussion that took place in my first course with manuel arturo abreu, ZOMBIE: Fear of a Black Republic. This was a reach back in time as my email application was sent on August 30th of 2020. I watched and listened intently to what is now more than a two-year-old conversation with a gorgeous spread of themes including, of course, zombies, as well as spirits, unveiling, mystery, dreams, individual and collective wounding, children, and much more.

As I watched our conversation, I was reintroduced to a familiar sensation: the mind/body/spirit churning that, for me, only arrives when people gather to give a question a rite of passage. I soon found myself on my feet, needing to move... needing to match inner movements with outer.

I remembered how this conversation, like many, many others we had in our time together was alive, or undead.

I'll relay to you all an anecdote shared in our final course discussion from another student (pregnant at the time). Towards the end of our discussion, they explained that they weren't saying much because their baby was kicking strongly throughout our conversation (and perhaps in response to it). This participant also shared a recent dream of theirs (a common ZOMBIE course occurrence). In this particular dream, they brought their baby home, which they said had "*really* big eyes," and after breastfeeding, the baby walked outside and flew into the air.

This is what I needed to share with you all. I believe this dream gestures toward the experience of manuel's coursework in a way that a more typical course description would fail to.

I understand that one of our themes for today is "playing at living." Through dreams, this baby was doing just that. When I think of making space, when I think of home school, when I think of students and artists like you all, I think of this big-eyed dream baby being cared for, being allowed to fly freely.

RAHEL AIMA & KAMEELAH JANAN RASHEED

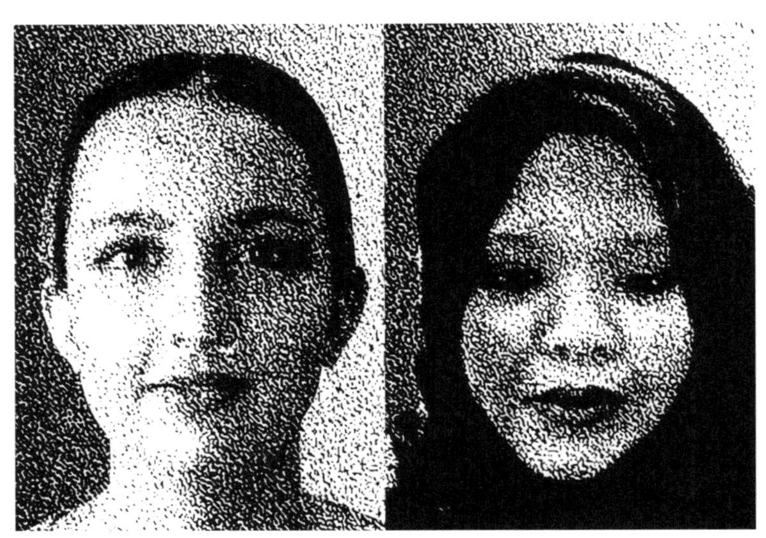

On Defying Existing Models for Institution Building

Writer rahel aima interviews learner and artist Kameelah Janan Rasheed about leaking, diacritics, and institutional kegels.

This conversation between rahel aima and Kameelah Janan Rasheed happened over Zoom in March of 2023. It has been edited for length and clarity.

Kameelah Janan Rasheed

The leak and membranes that don't fully hold the thing that is intended are really interesting in terms of the boundary between disciplines, between ideas, between myself and the rest of the world. How might the concept of leakiness be a framework to think through defying existing models for institution building and unlearning together?

rahel aima

I'm curious about what co-education looks like: it's still different in texture, in timbre from co-learning. Maybe it's about intention or the force behind the gesture. Learning can be so ambient. We get socialized, we learn from the environment, from many things around us. We can learn from animals. We're not necessarily actively educated by animals.

KJR

Just going through daily life, we may observe how a plant grows towards the light and understand phototropism. We may not have the word for it, but we understand that relationship between the plant and the light to be something particular. And we may not codify it or put it somewhere in a concrete manner, but it's still percolating, it's still within our network or hypertext. I really like this idea of learning as a space of embracing the ephemeral in the ambient, and education in a lot of ways, being this more formalized process of trying to pull all these things out of the air that are swirling around you, atmospherically.

I'm really interested in what gets lost in that transfer because learning, in a lot of ways, is ambient. But at the same time, institutions desire evidence of learning: how do we make space for the ambient? Actions of puncture allow for a little bit to leak out for something else to happen.

RA

Well, it's not necessarily positive. Because there is a lot of ambient learning that happens in institutions, and it's behavioral, it's telling the kid to not touch the artwork. The word I want to use is training, a repetition of gestures.

In your most recent newsletter there's this really beautiful phrase quoted, "No knowledge is complete until it passes through my body." I've been thinking about muscle memory recently, and also musical notation. You learn things by doing them again and again. But maybe it's also about the intensity, the dynamic marking in a way. So if you were to notate these different modes of learning or education as a graphic score, how would you connote things like pitch and tone, but also the accent or the shape of the things?

KJR

There's a bunch of things that are happening in my brain right now, and the thing that's coming up actually is about Arabic and diacritical marks. But before I say that, it makes me very excited because I have been thinking about scores in relation to syllabi and curriculum.

At CUNY Graduate Center they republish archives and re-contextualize them in these small booklets. There's one on Audre Lorde's teaching materials. And the editors who put this together, they have this really beautiful quote, Miriam Atkin and Iemanjá Brown. It reads, "Though these texts have the appearance of plans and instructions, they ultimately amount to points from which to converge, more than directions to follow. Taken together, they memorialize an activity that defied planning, re-constructing a teaching practice that saw the classroom as a collectively composed, gradually crafted commentary on the now."

In a lot of ways, syllabi, lesson plans, and curricular notes, are interesting technologies in that they are trying to map out, scope out, create a score around both cognitive movement as well as physical movement in a different environment. Having been a high school teacher and then coaching teachers for ten years after that, it's really interesting to watch just how frequently the thing that was planned just doesn't happen. A lot of times when I'm working with teachers I try to help them think about this as, "You're doing improv, you're literally doing improv. You're waiting for the word, you're waiting for that moment that will help you calibrate to figure out what's next."

So I really like this comparison to music notation. Because it gets at this relationship between body and mind in a more clear way. But I also think it speaks to teaching as a creative practice, as an art form. I know that not everyone believes that about their own or other people's practice. But I take it very seriously that what I'm doing is co-creating some type of art thing with the people that I have the privilege to share space with.

RA

I'm glad you brought up improvisation. I was thinking about scores that are followed versus scores that really set an ambiance, that create an environment or sonic space. But I'm also curious what you're thinking about diacritics.

KJR

I'm returning to Arabic study now by studying trilateral roots. Because the thing that I do enjoy about Arabic is that it feels very mathematical to me. So it feels easy to learn because I'm like, "Oh, these three letters, when seen together, have a general meaning. And the diacritical mark moves the meaning."

RA

Harakat. Yeah.

KJR

Yes, exactly. It means motion. There was something poetic about the idea that those trilateral roots mean something, but the thing that pushes it along in a sentence are the diacritical marks that give it locomotion so we can actually understand what's happening. I was working on this grant around machine learning text-to-image generation and had created this very rudimentary music notation system that basically used Arabic diacritical marks, the short vowels in addition to some of Ibn Arabi's cryptographic marks, to think about how to signal to an instrument player what to do.

I'm interested in the fusion of markings and language with music notation as a way to bridge our relationship between the musicality of sound and the musicality of a language that, in a lot of ways, functions from a set of consonants that are then moved along or given motion by vowels.

RA

I love the idea it's moving the word along. I'm seeing little caster wheels hitched underneath–something not meant to move all the time but maybe sometimes, you tilt it and it moves, which is a really nice way of thinking of not making something entirely mobile, but giving something the option to move. I like caster wheels because they don't always work. Sometimes the wheels are like, "No, we're stuck or we're going in all these different ways." But I'd like to return to leakiness too.

Education is something that contains learners. And something leaks when it's not contained, but something also leaks when it's not held. It's interesting to think about containment versus holding because those are different things. We can readily talk about holding each other without containing. I'm also wary of this kind of affective, emotive language. Yes, we're holding each other, but what does that mean? We're weaponizing, deploying language in these ways and not necessarily thinking about them.

KJR

It's almost like once something has become automatic or second nature for you, it feels less of a necessity to investigate the meanings because you already have embodied it, you're carrying an assumption of the meanings. And so there's no sense of second meanings.

RA

I love what you said about learning, something becoming automated, becoming embodied. What do diacritics do? It feels like they're doing the same thing as the beginning of a score, or if the markings were in a score, they're creating an atmosphere. Maybe it's a stretch to say it's world-building, but it's putting up some scenery in a way. And also, it's estranging in a way that's not negative. It feels like an ambient atmospheric thing that your body moves into. If we take the logic of grammatical cases as marked by Arabic diacritics or these other kinds of musical markings, the diacritics are marking relationships between things. This is the subject, this is the object, this is the actor, the acted upon.

It would be super interesting actually to invert those because if you were to transpose them to a classroom situation they're annotating hierarchical relationships. And it's funny that I'm like, "Oh, cases are vibes."

KJR

Yeah, I like the framing of them as vibes. In a given sentence, how do you mark or identify relationships between people, places, objects? And then how does that then get carried over into another setting? If you were to take a piece of acetate and lay it over a lesson, how might you use that to identify who's doing what?

My relationship to institutions a lot of times is understanding them not as this concretized, calcified institution that is unable to shift or be responsive, or improvise and collaborate with the folks who are engaged with it. The hard part for me is thinking about institutions that both have clarity in their values and ethics, while at the same time, being able to hop on a set of caster wheels as necessary. How do we keep the institution in motion? How do we provide opportunities for it to not calcify under the weight of its own values or the weight of its own beliefs about how something is supposed to function?

There's something about a leaky institution or a liquid or maybe a wet institution that isn't completely dried and calcified. Maybe it's not leakage. Maybe it's something about wetness or something about the thing sitting on the substrate in a way that makes it still possible for it to change.

RA

I love the idea of terroir, this idea that something reflects the acidity or chalkiness of the soil, the humidity or dryness in the air, whatever ambient atmospheric thing. And it makes me think about the institution that's not wet, but maybe humid, where there's moisture in a different form. It's the opposite of calcification. And also about what gets digested from the soil and air, what moves through the body, the person, the institution. But also, I'm thinking about the article that you sent over, on sensory gating. I had to look up what it was. ScienceDirect says "Sensory gating is a process by which irrelevant stimuli are separated from meaningful ones," which seems maybe a little heavy-handed to be a metaphor for what the institution does.

The institution: it's the turnstile gatekeeper, it selectively lets in things. The body does that too. A cell membrane will be like, "These are okay. These, no. Stop them at the walls." But the leak seems to override direction. It's going where it's not supposed to go, it's spreading if it's not contained. The leak seeps. I have a habit of not closing water bottles in my bag, and I'm always like, "Ah, this is spreading." The leak is absorbed by the fabric, by the air. It wants to be part of something else in a way, maybe.

KJR

I really love this notion that the leak wants to find another space for belonging. And I think about the number of times, like you, that I've left a water bottle in my bag and it's leaked all over my notes. It causes this blurring. And at first, it's quite frustrating. But then, there's sometimes these really beautiful things that happen because of that moment of contamination, or because of that moment of merging of surfaces.

And the sensory gating, learning that I have ADHD was really funny because part of the process for that is all these things that are around containment of that leakage. While sometimes it is overwhelming, I actually quite enjoy what I call being able to collect dirty data. It's the stuff that no one else is taking in because it can't be assimilated into their brain for a particular purpose. But the way that I'm processing the world, perceptually, is that I'm taking it all in. And I end up making a lot of use of that dirty data. And so there's something also beautiful for me about this bridge between policing cognitive functions around sensory gating.

I like the idea of an institution that has leaky or poor sensory gating. Not that I want the institution to be distracted from its own purposes, but it's not automatically filtering out things because they seem odd or don't fit into a template. That stage of pre-sorting just eliminates a lot of really interesting stuff. There's, of course, the highly technical understanding of dirty data, and the data janitors who are supposed to go back in and clean all the data up to make it not dirty and assimilable. And I'm really interested in that.

To what extent can an institution engage in research practices or expansion processes that engage with dirty data as an ethos? Maybe if I'm trying to build this learning institution, I am talking to a geologist because maybe something will come from that conversation. Or maybe I am talking to a kindergarten teacher in Uganda because maybe something will come from that conversation. But widening the scope of what we consider to be legitimate knowledge around what we learned, connect to, and make sense of is part of our work.

And then the last thing I'll say is the humidity thing hit me in the chest, because there's something about humidity as being both present and not present, both a burden but also appreciated all at the same time. The other thing you had mentioned around soil that was exciting for me was that you're right, it's not about wet because I think that that state of matter is too loose. It's almost about a substance that can both hold and release moisture as needed.

Maybe institutions might need to think about themselves in relation to soil. What does it mean to be soil? Not metaphorically in the sense of "we are grounded and we are in the earth and we are organic and we care," but soil in that "we can both hold and release." These opposite motions are necessary because you must release.

That's part of learning. You must gather, but you also must ungather. Because sometimes we hold onto things as individuals and institutions that are not healthy for us because we're used to the accumulation under capitalism, you just gather and collect things. But what would it mean for an institution to lean towards an ethos of soil? There's a whole world within that soil, there's a whole ecosystem, a whole set of relations within that soil that make all of those functions that are holding and releasing possible. I'm really happy you said soil and I'm really happy you said humidity. That shifted so much.

RA

This is making me think literally of institutional kegels as a kind of strengthening exercise—and holding and releasing as opposed to opening and closing, which is very different. But I'm thinking too of data as refining raw ore—a quite toxic process—before it gets run through the institution of the database, the Excel, the SQL, the whatever. You delete repetitions. You're like, "These things we think are the same, and we're going to merge them." You merge and you remove duplicates. And that's really what the institution does. It comes down to this process of representation or like, "This will do for this, this will do for this, this will do for this." The DEI of museums in particular...

KJR

I really like thinking about dirty data outside of the context of just data itself because it provides such a generative language around the ways in which we police what is possible when we don't have the ability, interest, time, or wherewithal to do the extra work needed to make something legible in a particular way. The problem with processes like deduplication is that they don't take into consideration how nuance is often built under the surface and that there's an interiority to both people and to processes that need to be honored that dirty data cleaning systems can't figure out.

And so I think about institutions in relation to efficiency and what it means to slow down. What does it mean to organize my institution around a longer time period for processing? We all need processing time, and we all need space to actively engage with the dirty data that is ourselves.

We do this every single day. We're having an emotion that we can't translate or make sense of.

So we push it aside instead of just sitting with it and being like, "What is happening?" We're like, "We don't have time. Moving on." And so I think it's how to listen, making sure that your antenna is not only picking up what has been identified as signal, but an institutional antenna that picks up the signal and the noise all the time and has meaningful processes for sorting. And by sorting, I don't mean discarding, but actually processing the information in the community with an awareness that there may be something that lives under something else, under another layer that we may have to work a little harder to find.

RA

In the construction industry they use these semi-permeable meshes called geotextiles, which hold and release at the same time, essentially. What they do is they keep solid matter in, mostly soil and rocks, and they let water flow. Groundwater welling actually is interesting as opposed to leaking because it's a different direction of motion. Blooming versus leaking, like mold.

KJR

The geotextiles, I'm probably going to end up in a four-hour rabbit hole. The images almost look like they have found a weaving pattern where these materials can dance together in a particular way to allow opposite simultaneous motion and movement. And there's something so deeply poetic and beautiful about that.

SHANI PETERS, AMERICAN ARTIST & ALLIE LINN

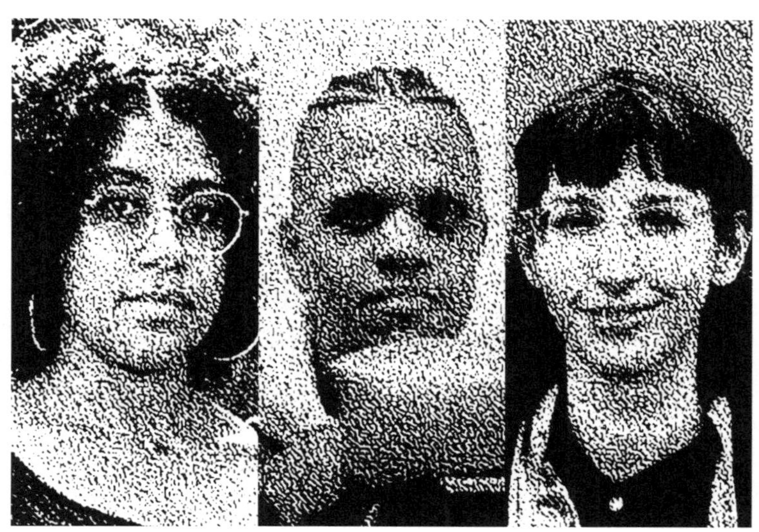

On What a School Can Be

Artist and writer Allie Linn interviews artists and educators Shani Peters and American Artist about the importance of rethinking traditional educational models, cultivating community, and inspiring curiosity within the classroom.

This is a transcript of a conversation between Shani Peters, American Artist, and Allie Linn that took place via Zoom in June of 2022. It has been lightly edited for length. This conversation was originally commissioned by United States Artists for their digital publication New Suns: Listening with Artists.

Allie Linn

To start from the beginning, what was your relationship to school and schooling growing up? I'm thinking about school generally here; this could be specific memories of educational spaces or the spaces you remember being the biggest catalysts for learning for you.

American Artist

A lot of my positive experiences of school I associate with specific teachers or educators that allowed for space where I could be creative or explore what I wanted. I remember a lot of the more determined parts of schooling being really boring and not really generative for wanting to learn. I remember that specifically about learning history. I found it extremely boring and it wasn't until I was an adult that I found out how it could be interesting. So I feel like a lot of my education as a young person was about finding chances where I could be creative or throw myself and my energy into something that felt inspiring to me, even if that wasn't necessarily what my experience was designed to be.

Shani Peters

Two things come to mind. One is in terms of going to school, like leaving my house and going to school. My older brother is super smart. He was valedictorian and he didn't go but he got into Harvard. He speaks, like, five languages now. So it was double-edged. He paved a nice, smooth path for me going to school. All of my teachers had already had him, so they were like, “Oh, okay, so you’re good.” It was probably easier than it could have been for me. Me, I did alright, in part thanks to that eased relationship, that well-buttered road. But I definitely think I’m dyslexic; I’ve never been diagnosed with it, but I struggled with reading early on and always had more academic challenges in school than my brother did. So even though I did well in school and was always perceived as smart internally and within my family, I never felt like I was on that same level. That was an insecurity in high school and younger, and so finding my way to the discipline of art and learning history through art, versus through those boring history classes, was watershed for me because it showed me that there was a space where I could excel. There was a space where that came naturally, where I wasn’t fighting to be on that level. That was a big attraction with art.

I think the other thing that’s significant about my understanding of school early on is that my dad—he’s retired now—was a Black Studies professor. We think about this a lot now with the work Joseph Cuillier and I are doing in The Black School. We think a lot about where Black people get our knowledge of Black history, and it tends to land at home. It tends to be that if you got it early on, before you came into a Black Studies department, you probably got it from a family member, and my dad being a professor in the field made that even more articulated for me. From as early as I can remember, I was getting whole Black history lessons and a whole clearly identified education from home.

AL

You both named finding the parts of schooling that were inspiring in order to better navigate through the parts that were less accessible or that didn't resonate as much. And now each of you has stewarded an alternative school—Shani, from the founding of The Black School, and American, during a moment of reorganization for the School of Poetic Computation—amongst many other teaching roles. What has the process of building and rebuilding spaces for learning and shared knowledge been like? What has informed your imagining of what a school can be?

SP

We started the organization in New York. I'm from Michigan and Joseph is from New Orleans, but we met in New York. We started working there, where space is just such a premium, and I won't say impossible—people have figured it out, The School of Poetic Computation has figured it out, which I was amazed by when I learned that, especially in that part of town—but we definitely took a lot of lessons from a New York organization, The Laundromat Project, who I worked with from the very beginning. I saw the way the organization grew and was familiar with how it was conceived at its founding, which was by a woman named Risë Wilson, who worked for foundations and saw a lot of organizations spending all of their operating budgets and going under because they were having to focus more on just keeping lights on than their programming. She thought of a way to have programming without that overhead, and it was imagining laundromats as these built-in, pre-existing community centers to be activated by programming.

So we took that approach to the ideas that we had for programming for The Black School. We dreamed it up. We collaborated with folks. We created lessons, syllabi, and then just took it to places that had space and people of multiple generations. That worked in ways we planned and ways we didn't and gave us a lot of opportunities to experiment and try different things and learn as we built. That was definitely thinking of a space for learning and something that is not about physical, tangible space, but more about the people and how people can transform whatever confines or spaces they're in.

The biggest disadvantage of all of that is that it's hard to sustain relationships with people because you're going to a different place all the time. There were some advantages and a really significant disadvantage, and with both of us being educators and people deeply invested in seeing tangible outcomes from the ideas that we come up with, we both had a desire to work more sustainably and rooted in one place. A very big part of what we're trying to do is create a new model. It is institution-building, but institutions don't have to look like the institutions that we've had, so how do we learn and grow and propose something different?

AL

I'm curious how that translates for you, American, as someone who didn't necessarily found School for Poetic Computation, but, as you mentioned, you have begun to steward it with some other members of SFPC. What has that experience been like?

AA

In the space that we're in now, during the summer of 2020, around the time that there were protests in response to the murder of George Floyd and a lot of institutions were asking for accountability within their institutions for various forms of injustice or inequity. Similarly, a lot of stewards and teachers of SFPC felt like, "Okay, how can our institution be better and be more accountable to those people that are participating and also to the stewards and teachers, as well?" A lot of us decided that we wanted to have more stake in the school and in designing what it can be and the values that it is going to represent. We laid that out and put ourselves forward.

Since then, we've stepped into these leadership roles and the past leadership has been helping us transition into these roles, but they're no longer affiliated with the school. Now it's seven of us as co-directors designing what the school is going to be. The other co-directors were past students of mine or assistant teachers or other fellow teachers, so my understanding of this school feels directly out of what has happened in our classroom experiences. It doesn't feel as bureaucratic and hegemonic as the university. It feels like something that's coming more out of what we want the experience of study to be, first and foremost, and how we want to treat people and each other, and then everything else sort of happens around that.

It's constantly trying to recalculate how this all fits together because it's so atypical, but it feels really important.

SP

Atypical is what we need. I think I'm so in the weeds of what we're doing now that I'll start answering questions and skip over a lot, and the basis is like, schools are trash. Burn it down from Pre-K to PhD. It's not where it's at. Rethinking all of it from top to bottom. That's the first step and then everything else goes from that.

AL

You mentioned teaching at other universities, American, and I'm sure you both have interfaced with a lot of different types of institutions: schools, museums, non-profits. I'm curious if that work has informed your work with The Black School and with the School for Poetic Computation, too.

AA

Myself and the other co-directors, many of us have taught in universities and worked with these more established institutions. We all have a certain amount of skepticism and criticality towards those, and though I still feel very dependent on those work-wise, SFPC allows us to have a space where we can experiment with what a different model could be. I do feel like a lot of the positive or optimistic energy I have around what study can be goes towards SFPC and similarly, I feel like that is starting to seep into the space I hold in my classes, even if that is in the university. I want to protect the students or have a special engagement with them, even if the overall structure feels violent, for lack of a better word.

SP

All of my experiences inform what we're doing now. The positive and the negative experiences all inform this work positively. You learn what you don't want to do, what you don't want to replicate. When I think about teaching and the kind of teaching that I love, it is primarily with younger people, and that's primarily because of the inequities that exist in our society and who winds up being able to afford going to college. I definitely bring a ton from the experiences of working in middle schools and high schools, and seeing the difference between going into the built environment of a cinderblock school with no windows in the Bronx, and how the students respond to me and to the lesson in that space, versus being able to come into the Bronx Museum, whose building is partly renovated, and the education space in the new side is this beautiful modern architecture with floor-to-ceiling windows and the light coming in. Similarly, the first place I started teaching was Harlem Textile Works, which no longer exists. There's a real estate office running out of that space now. But it was a beautiful space specifically made for art-making and had a whole different impact on the way young people interface with the idea of making art. That has taught me a lot.

Getting a teaching position at Parsons or the private schools that are able to pay more of a living wage is very, very difficult, but eventually I was able to get some of those positions. I taught at Parsons and Pratt and it was super refreshing in some ways, to see what it's like to have those resources, to see what it's like for students to have the amount of credit hours dedicated to the classroom to really be able to explore things. It was amazing and also, simultaneously, deeply unsatisfying, because the inequity is right there. All of the classes that I was ever invited to teach were studying the inequity of how fucked up it all is, and the student population is represented in this room to no fault of these individuals there. They're just moving through life in the world they were born into, but this is the problem. So you become a part of replicating it.

It's very empowering to have intimately been within those positions and to see how flawed they are, because they look so prestigious and they create this impostor syndrome you hear people talk so much about, this sense that things are just impossible and not attainable. Privilege creates this dynamic where people actually have less practice with managing difficult situations than the "underprivileged." So in that way the "underprivileged" are actually more skilled and capable of taking on the challenges that exist in building something. So even when it's overwhelming, it all makes me feel capable, because I've seen what it takes and how much money folks have in one space and how little they're able to actually do with it.

AL

You were also beginning to describe the physical architecture of some of those early educational spaces, and you were pointing to things like cinderblock walls and windows. I've been thinking about architecture as such a big piece of this conversation, too.

SP

Yeah, I think about the building all the time. I've Zoomed with architects every two weeks for two years now. I think it's a huge piece. I think the overwhelming idea that we're moving with goes back to your first question about the relationship of school growing up and the relationship of Black people having to get at things ourselves, so that's often coming from home. We're definitely thinking about how to make a space feel more like home than a typical built school. City College is this beautiful Gothic historic campus, but the student admin building, one of the newer buildings on the campus, was built by prison architects. Everybody knows it, it's clear as day. There are stenciled classroom numbers to say what room number this is. It's this giant stencil you see if you're watching *The Wire* or a TV show set.

There are so many of these schools that are literally built to look like prisons, for economic reasons, whatever the case. Of course, those are not inspiring curiosity in the people that step through it. So how do we inspire curiosity? And how do we make people feel comfortable? How do we let people know that this is truly a different type of space that we're trying to create here that is for you and of you and not antagonistic to you?

AA

Yeah, I completely agree, and I do think a lot about how the architecture of a lot of schools and universities reproduces this sort of prison architecture and its security. Students can't access the campus or they're policed or they're asked to show their IDs and all these different things. It's already a place a lot of people don't want to go because they feel like they have to go, and then on top of that, you feel policed within your own learning environment, so I echo this sentiment that the school should feel like home or a place that's comfortable or inspiring.

I think that's definitely something we've thought a lot about at SFPC. We formerly had a space at the Westbeth Building, an arts building in lower Manhattan, and a central part of that space was a kitchen. Typically, the students would take several classes at the same time, and it would be a set cohort of students that would all be participating together. After class, they would cook meals together and hang out. That felt like a central part of the study, and they would talk through things they were struggling with together through that time, as well. It created this thing that felt very comfortable: the study could seep beyond just what's happening in the classroom, where stuff is sort of dumped on you, but then you can unpack it with other students that are at the same level as you. You don't feel intimidated or some type of way, and it actually becomes an enjoyable experience.

Through the pandemic we did move into a virtual model, and that has allowed its own sort of benefits, I think. In one sense, we've been able to offer classes beyond New York, far beyond New York. People from many different countries have been able to participate, which is really exciting. For that reason, I don't think we will ever not have some virtual part to it, because of what that's allowed us to do. But we aspire to have a space again, a physical space where we can invite people to come and commune and make food and think about and study ideas together in a way that does feel comfortable, fulfilling, and exciting.

AL

Yeah, all of those spaces on the margins, outside of the official classroom or teaching space, are so important for that kind of continued conversation. Having those spaces to cook together and just be human together. To close out, I'd love to hear what questions or attitudes or mindsets you try to instill in your students. What do you hope for your students to take away from your teaching?

SP

We always start with these questions: What do you love about your community? And what do you want to change about your community? We first ask, "What do you love?" because there are things to love. The inequity is real. Poverty leads to a whole lot of messed up circumstances. No shit. The poverty is the problem. Fix the poverty and then you don't have to treat people like this. Even within the circumstances that so many people without money find themselves, there is a lot to love in this country. It's still home. It's still family. It's still a community. We want to focus on whatever folks' answers are to that. Start with questions and start with opening up the space. What we're going to do, we figure out together. We are always trying to strike that balance and remind people that there is the option of increasing what's good as a solution to removing what is wrong. Those questions are really key. I think the other key is just creating a space where people can see and feel that they really do have some wherewithal to change what they want to change, be it on a personal internal level or societal, local, community level, and so on.

We definitely build so much of what we do from bell hooks' *Teaching to Transgress* and

Paulo Freire's *Pedagogy of the Oppressed.* Simple ideas—we don't have to reinvent wheels. People have been living through a lot of toxic, awful shit for a very long time, and so the models are there. We didn't start off thinking this, but we've found that whatever it is we've wanted to do, even the most abstract, random, one-off ideas, like we wanted to make tetrahedral kites, and we were looking at Edison's kites, and as we looked at these photos from Edison's kite collective—there was actually a group—there was this Black guy, this random Black guy. Who's he? What's his story? Black people have already done everything. We have done the things. They've been burned down, they've been suppressed.

So whatever it is you want to do, there is a precedent for it, Black or otherwise. There's a precedent for it and that can give you a roadmap of what to do, but it also can inspire and can show you that the narratives that we're taught about who's capable and who's not are just so false.

DANA KOPEL

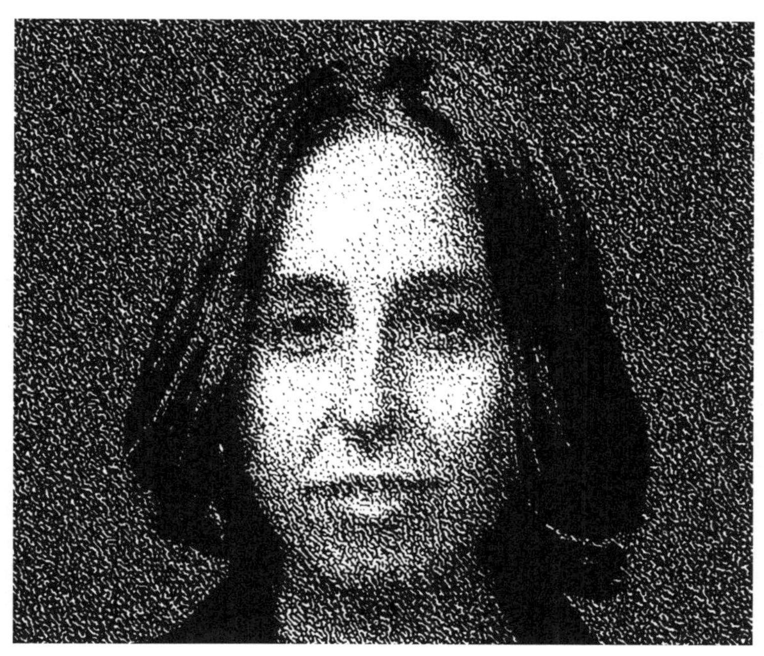

Museum Strikes and the Limits of Art Institutions.

On September 26, 2022, workers at the Philadelphia Museum of Art walked off the job. They'd unionized in August 2020 with AFSCME Local 397, winning their election with an overwhelming 89 percent "yes" vote after leadership refused to voluntarily recognize their union—despite the disruption of the Covid-19 Pandemic and the museum's decision to lay off eighty-five workers only two days before the vote. Contract negotiations began in October of that year, an uphill battle against management's intransigence and apparent disdain for the needs of their staff. In August 2022, the union filed eight Unfair Labor Practice charges with the National Labor Relations Board, accusing the museum of breaking federal labor law by interfering with workers' legal right to organize. They held a strike vote on August 30; not a single worker voted no. And they held a daylong "warning strike" on September 16, an intimation of their collective power and the loss that their withheld labor represents.

This narrative of organizing, escalation, and pushback from management is a familiar story to many museum workers—and many workers in other fields—who have been involved in unionization efforts in the past few years. As a former editor at the New Museum and one of the New Museum Union's organizers, and then bargaining committee members, I could certainly relate—not just to the broad outlines of the process but to some of the minute details, too. Nicole Cook, the PMA's program manager for graduate academic partnerships and a union trustee, told *Philadelphia* magazine shortly after the end of the strike that they had spent "two years at the bargaining table, going back and forth making mountains out of molehills, like the weeks spent on something as simple as where we could put union materials on a bulletin board."[1] We'd had a weeks-long bulletin board fight at the New Museum, too. First management refused to let us put

1. Sarah Jordan, "After Last Year's Labor Battle, Will the Art Museum Come Back Stronger?," *Philadelphia*, January 1, 2023, https://www.phillymag.com/news/2023/01/28/art-museum-strike/.

up bulletin boards in staff break areas altogether, then they conceded on one in the office but wouldn't allow another in the break area for front-of-house staff (likely because that space was shared by unionized and nonunion staff, and they didn't want the latter to get any ideas about organizing themselves). The union-busting playbook for museums is fundamentally the same, whether it's Morgan Lewis (PMA), Proskauer (New Museum, MoMA), or another white-shoe law firm behind it. Beyond the typical claims of poverty ("we can't afford this") and bureaucracy ("this makes it harder for us to work together") deployed by employers across industries, museums and their lawyers tend to lean on institutions' nonprofit status and weaponize employees' passion for their work by insinuating, for instance, that wage increases would be taken away from limited funds for artists' projects.

But the PMA strike was different. Since the start of the recent museum union movement in early 2019, only a few unions at cultural institutions—the Museum of Fine Arts Boston, MASS MoCA—have gone on one-day walkouts, important actions that are limited in time and often, as a result, in both risk and effectiveness. At the New Museum, the union held a strike vote (96 percent yes, another strong majority) but managed to settle its first contract without actually striking. Before September 2022, there hadn't been a major museum strike in over two decades, when the Museum of Modern Art's professional staff union struck for four and a half months. The PMA strike was historic. It was a powerful and necessary escalation in the recent wave of museum worker struggle. It was also part of a broader wave of strike actions over the past few years, from digital media workers to coal miners and from Instacart shoppers to teachers and graduate students. And after nineteen days, it worked: the PMA Union won a contract that featured major wage increases, reduced healthcare costs, improved parental leave, and more. As the saying goes, "Direct action gets the goods."

I followed along online from the West Coast a little wistfully, wishing I could join the picketers on the museum's massive front steps. But strikes don't only happen on the picket line, as the PMA Union reminded me. Community support is integral, whether it's contributing to hardship funds, participating in the social reproduction of the strike (buying or cooking food for the strikers, cleaning up each day), or dragging an employer on social media. During the PMA strike, workers and supporters–myself proudly included–flooded the PMA's Twitter replies and Instagram posts with comments admonishing them for union-busting and expressing support for striking staff. Under a handful of tone-deaf graphic posts shared during the strike that read, "THE MUSEUM IS OPEN TODAY. We are committed to serving our community as we continue to negotiate in good faith toward a fair and appropriate new labor agreement" ran a steady stream of refusals to cross the picket line, statements of solidarity, and rat emojis. One Instagram user thoughtfully wrote, "Actions speak louder than words! If you're truly committed to 'serving the community,' you'll realize that workers at the PMA are part of that community too–the part that cares enough to give you their time, labor, and experience. Support your workers and work with the union. #solidarity." Another simply wrote, "no." Eventually, the museum disabled comments.

+++

How do you think about art institutions without immediately thinking about their limitations, their failures? As a worker in an institution–and not only in an art institution, though that is the kind I am most familiar with–you come up against its limits all the time: what you shouldn't say and who you shouldn't say it to, what your position in the hierarchy allows and what it prohibits, how the institution causes harm and how you are punished if you speak up about it. You come up against "no" and "not now" and, especially, "there's no money for that." Formal complaints lead nowhere. Advocating for yourself tends to lead nowhere, too. The recent museum union movement marks a recognition of this painful truth and a response to it. What we can't accomplish alone, as individuals–livable wages, affordable healthcare, equitable leave policies, a fair process for addressing grievances–we can win collectively.

People generally start working in museums because they care about art. (As countless self-serious curators have pointed out, the Latin root for "curate" is *curare*, meaning "to care"; I'd love to know if that care extends to the staff working under them.) Probably because of this, though also for strategic reasons, the language of care shows up everywhere in museum union communications. I should know; I'm responsible for some of it. When my colleagues and I first publicly announced our intent to unionize at the New Museum, we wrote about our "pride in the Museum's legacy" and our "commitment" to its mission. PMA workers, in their first press release about the union effort, wrote, "We are unionizing out of love for the arts, the museum, and each other." Other examples abound in text shared by unionizing museum workers, nonprofit staff, and, increasingly, employees at "enlightened" corporations like Starbucks, REI, and Trader Joe's. For museum unions, this is effective in several ways: it foregrounds workers' commitment to the institutions they work in; it acknowledges the perceived privilege of having these jobs while gently pushing against the idea that such privilege compensates for low pay and bad conditions; and it makes clear that any hostility that arises is coming from management, since the union's tone is caring and almost conciliatory. I also have no doubt that for many museum workers, that care is genuine. The problem is that it is fundamentally one-sided.

During their strike, PMA workers mobilized care pointedly and effectively. They had walked out shortly before installation of the museum's major Henri Matisse exhibition was set to begin. (Picket signs read, "No contract, no Matisse!") Rather than using that time pressure to quickly settle a contract, PMA leadership hired scabs to fill in for art handlers on strike. As the union pointed out, this not only disrespected the specialized labor of striking staff; it also put extremely valuable paintings at risk. In a Twitter thread on October 5, the PMA Union account wrote,

> While they leave the professional art handling staff of the museum out in the cold, [PMA CEO] Sasha Suda and [COO] Bill Petersen [are] bringing in scabs to hang Matisse? How much are they paying? What hardware are they using? The long-term damage to this museum [is] unfathomable.... Lenders who are trusting the @philamuseum with their Matisses deserve better. Do they know who's handling their paintings? Their credentials? We are ashamed that @philamuseum 's CEO, COO, and board seem to care so little for the relationships we've spent years building.

Here, again, workers' care is both sincere and strategic. In addition to demonstrating their concern for the museum, even while recognizing that concern as one-sided, the tweets reflect an attempt to mobilize powerful museum stakeholders who do not generally support unions–wealthy collectors and museum executives–by emphasizing those stakeholders' investment (literal and figurative) in the careful handling of their artworks. Further, the tweets suggest workers' ambivalence about the institution's capacity to care: they seem to reify the fiction of the ethical museum while turning that fiction against itself–or rather, against the museum that maintains and profits from it. "Oh you're a *good* museum?" the workers ask. "Prove it."

Looking at some of the discourse around the 2000 MoMA strike reveals notable similarities in how union members talk about their work and their care for the institution. In an article from *Artforum*'s September 2000 issue, Daniel B. Schneider describes the striking workers as "quick to proclaim their respect for the museum's programs and collections." He quotes a research assistant in the department of painting and sculpture and member of the union's bargaining team, Carina Evangelista, describing the endemic problems of museum work, which remain discouragingly familiar more than two decades later: "It is such a reflection of the art profession at large, this pervasive notion that only privileged individuals work in the art world.... When I hear that some people on the staff can't afford a phone, it's just not excusable."[2] The strike, which lasted 134 days and affected a bargaining unit of 250 people, significantly improved these conditions. Among the union's wins were major wage increases, the right to bargain over health coverage, and the right to return to one's position if one was furloughed during the museum's five-year closure for renovation and expansion. Yet perhaps the most significant victory was what's known as a closed shop, in which anyone hired into a union-eligible position automatically becomes a union member. By contrast, before fall 2000, MoMA's union operated as an open shop, much as unions in many states in the US South and West–where conservative state governments have passed deceptively named "right to work" laws to weaken union density and worker power–are still forced to do. That most newly formed museum unions are closed shops (other than those in "right to work" states, where it remains illegal) is a testament, in part, to MoMA's powerful precedent. The PMA's hard-won wall-to-wall unit–that is, their union contains eligible staff across the entire museum, not

2. Daniel B. Schneider, "The MoMA Strike," *Artforum*, September 2000, https://www.artforum.com/print/200007/the-moma-strike-32165.

3. Jason Simon, *Festschrift for an Archive*, 2012, artist's book, 11.

just certain departments—represents, I hope, another powerful precedent: breaking down divides between what's seen as professional and blue-collar work within museums, bringing workers together to strengthen all of us.

+++

In October 2019, I bought a $300 book. It wasn't the best financial decision—among my friends and family, I'm not known for good financial decisions; I guess working in art institutions would count among the many bad ones—but we had just ratified our first contract at the New Museum two weeks earlier and I was riding high on the raises we'd secured, on a prolonged lack of sleep, and on what I'd later come to recognize as clinical trauma. The book, which I treasure, is an artwork by Jason Simon. Titled *Festschrift for an Archive* (2012), it compiles an interview between the artist and Mary Corliss, the former associate curator of MoMA's Film Stills Archive, alongside the full text of the National Labor Relations Board's two decisions regarding layoffs at MoMA following the strike there.

MoMA made Corliss, a vocal union supporter who had been at the museum for decades and participated in the union recognition strikes in the early 1970s, a casualty of the 2000 strike. They laid off her and her colleague at the Film Stills Archive, both leaders during the strike, and moved the Archive to rural Pennsylvania, effectively closing it. Even from this vantage point, care for the Archive, for the work she did at MoMA, suffuses the interview. She reflects, "What bothers me is that there's no conscience, no morality to what they've done. There's no making a wrong right here. And again, it's not about me, because I'm out of it. I'm gone there. But they still have this majestic collection that is inaccessible and I wonder how, or even if, it's being preserved and maintained. That's what angers me more than anything."[3] The NLRB decisions that follow offer little more hope. While they first found

MoMA guilty of unfair labor practices and called for back pay for Corliss and her colleague, the subsequent decision—the result of MoMA appealing the original—did not find "antiunion animus" in MoMA's actions.[4] The judge dismissed the complaint.

Despite the dry, bureaucratic language of the NLRB decisions, *Festschrift for an Archive* has a heaviness to it, a sense of loss. The institutions we care for, that we invest our lives and passions in, don't give a shit about us. And the state—here manifested in the NLRB and US labor law—won't protect us. These can be painful truths, but they should, I hope, lead us to each other, to collective organizing and solidarity. Each copy of *Festschrift for an Archive* contains a still from a film about labor tucked into its front inner cover; in mine, it's an image from Barbara Kopple's 1990 *American Dream*, a documentary about the failed strike at Hormel Foods in Austin, Minnesota, in 1985–86. Over the duration of the strike, which began in response to significant cuts to workers' wages and benefits, Hormel replaced the vast majority of the workers who walked out. The company even leased half of its factory to another firm that paid only $6.50 an hour, far less than the $10.69 the workers struck to maintain. Yet in the film still, Ray Rogers, a union strategy consultant who has come from New York to support the strike, stands in the dark among the striking workers, his arms spread wide and his mouth open as though he's in the middle of a picket line chant. The fight continues. It has to.

4. Simon, *Festschrift*, 61.

LYNNE YUN, YATÚ ESPINOSA & NORM O’HAGAN

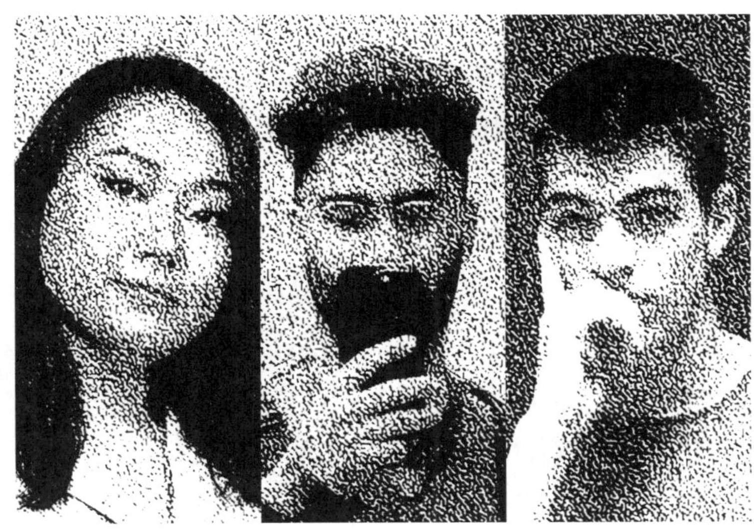

On Reframing the Context of Learning

Type designer and educator Lynne Yun in conversation with artist-founders Yatú Espinosa and Norm O'Hagan about creating the educational environments we wish we experienced and crafting the affordances from which learning can occur.

This conversation between Lynne Yun, Yatú Espinosa, and Norm O'Hagan happened over Zoom in March of 2023. It has been edited for length and clarity.

Lynne Yun

I went through SFPC's Code Societies program in 2018, and then the residency program that fall. That was my first foray into an alternative space. I hesitate a little bit in saying the word "alternative" because it makes it feel like it's self-marginalizing. At the same time, that was my first experience that wasn't in a formal learning institution that was framed as a learning space. From there, I started to expand my idea of what learning was. Learning is something that can happen when you're just making food with people in a space or just talking to people about how their day went.

That was also an unlearning experience because it was challenging my notions of what an educational space is, what a learning space is, and who gets to teach and who gets to learn. In that scenario, the hierarchies of these relationships start to break down a little bit. Some years later, I started an online school called Type Electives.

This school is rooted in a lot of the things that I learned at SFPC, in the sense of who gets to teach, who gets to learn, and how do we frame those relationships? In terms of practicality, we have been trying to have our faculty made up of people who have been wanting to teach but were having a hard time finding their spots in the traditional system. Especially for people of color and queer identities who have faced a lot of difficulty in breaking into traditional learning spaces because they don't have a certain advanced institutional degree, or maybe their learning has been from places that formal institutions do not recognize. This is an attempt for us to really tap into those people and create these spaces, "the by us for us" ethos, so to speak.

Norm O'Hagan

Similarly for me, when I was going through SFPC, it was a second chance at school or learning in general and for seeing it as a different type of environment. I remember one of the big things early on, during one of the first days of Code Societies with Melanie Hoff, was talking about the different models of hierarchies for learning. That idea of an independent school that doesn't have all of the ways and processes of being that the bigger institutions have was super exciting. I had gone through SFPC after we had started our educational institution, LRFT, which is short for Leave Room for Thoughts.

Yatú Espinosa

Leave Room for Thoughts really came about after Norm and I organized and attended several hackathons and realized that the tech DNA of hackathons really lended us to focus on the culture of startups. In that, as we were being nurtured, we lost sight of the artistic expression of creating something. Not even lost sight; I don't think we had the prescription to see it. Slowly and surely, we first started exploring design. Since design wasn't offered at our university, hackathons were really these environments for us to explore those different skill sets. Then through design, we also realized that we can make websites and they can be seen as art, rather than just utility.

At the core, as we started uncovering more and digging deeper, we realized that hackathons for us were really just alternative educational environments that our university wasn't able to provide, and we wanted to make one for ourselves. So we created our own month-long residency before entering into full-time jobs, and throughout that residency, we just found ourselves doing the same thing over again: having people come over to a space and helping them make things. At the crux was education. We wondered, "What if we made an educational institution?" That's what the art project ended up being, and as that has evolved, we formed principles around it.

NO

Space is a big one, and that's baked into the name of Leave Room for Thoughts. If spaces are set up in a way where there's a lot of affordances and tons of open room to use those affordances, then that can lead to a lot of learning and a lot of something that feels like an alternative to the structure, coursework, and syllabuses of traditional institutions, an alternative where one can find their own path. That feels like speculative fiction of an alternate world that could exist.

LY

When I was doing my master's at NYU Interactive Telecommunications Program, I was taking a class taught by Clay Shirky, and the topic was on online learning, which was very apt because this was a Zoom class during the pandemic summer of 2020. Talking about various modes of learning opened my eyes to how we are learning everything every single day. Maybe you have a favorite bodega or something, and one day you show up on Monday and they just happen to not be open. And in that little moment, you learn that they're not open on Mondays. That is a learning moment, although we probably never would consider that as one in the traditional sense.

I now often think about sharing space with people as an informal learning space. If you surround yourself with people that you admire and want to learn from, you're probably going to absorb little things just by observing or just being around them. It might be such a natural osmosis that it might not even register in your brain as learning with a capital L, but it's still very much a learning process.

YE

To add on to that, experience is one of the highest forms of discovery. We can speculate, or we can be told, but it's not until we go to that bodega and experience it for ourselves first hand that we know it is actually closed. We're always in the process of becoming, we're always in the process of learning.

Many people learn "on the job," but the office is a social construct. The school is also a social construct, and we've been exploring the notion of "schoolscapes." In the autumn of last year, we practiced schoolscaping by creating Campus Complex, which we identify as a newer circle of learning. A circle of learning doesn't need much, just an educator who has processes–through words, conversation, or a course–and a learner who's just curious and can go around and move freely, and those roles can be exchanged. If we can connect all these spaces that have different tools, we create a schoolscape that can become a new campus. Especially for those who have already graduated or for those who may not be getting the educational opportunities they hoped they would have at an institution that's been established for centuries.

LY

That reminds me of the concept of the Indigenous American medicine wheel, where people are going around and around in this big circle. Learning starts with anticipation, goes into curiosity, and then propels you into introspection. And then you integrate it back, and it starts again and again. That wheel is something that I always think about in the ways that I'm constructing learning spaces for myself and for others. The idea is that every time you go around this circle, you are progressing more and more to a higher state, if I may put it that way. It's very inspiring, the idea that the relationship between a learner and a teacher is actually one and the same, depending on where you are in that circle of learning. You can be both things; you can hold both things. It allows for more possibilities rather than, "I have already learned all the things, I am no longer a learner."

YE

Something to also call out is moving away from the word teacher and students and leaning more towards educator and learner. I find those words to be friendlier towards the fluidity of the moments that each role can have rather than the position they're in within the exchange of information.

Laurel Schwulst has this are.na channel called "Teaching is Creating Educational

Environments." It ties together with what we were discussing earlier with Leave Room for Thoughts, creating hackathons, and expanding into schoolscapes. The environments that we create, whether physically or digitally, are what are going to allow people to experience those moments of learning that you were describing. And in this case, it was just a city and a bodega. Our agency is really defined by the affordances around us. Our environment determines that, whether it's our interfaces at a digital level, or our surroundings on the physical.

LY

What have been the challenges that you have faced when you're actually trying to make this into a reality? Has there been a process of friction that you had to navigate?

YE

Education is inherently selfless. It can be common to discover that many people who are trying to create educational environments don't have the support they need in many areas, whether it's finances, labor, commitment, or resources in general. This is typically the case because it is considered to not be tangible in value, even though there is real value. Certifications are viewed as the closest it gets to tangibility, which, with time, have been proving themselves to not be that worthy.

NO

One of the challenges is that a lot of the resources are in walled gardens of the larger institutions. Access to those can be limited if you're not a part of the institution. Unless an initiative is directly tied to an organization that can sustain it, it can be really hard for it to survive over time. Especially within the typical institutional environment of the States. If you're trying to create an alternative initiative inside of a campus or within something that already exists, then a challenge is figuring out how to make that institution care about the initiative so that it'll be committed to ensuring that it sustains itself. Outside of that, it can also be challenging to find the momentum to keep the initiative going when there will always be so much gravity towards the existing educational institutions in terms of resources being poured into those.

LY

For myself and my co-founder Juan Villanueva, some of the biggest challenges in creating our new school Type Electives have been in trying to imagine a new space while creating support systems that we did not have while teaching for traditional institutions. We've taught for large institutions such as the Letterform Archive, Parsons School of Design, and the School of Visual Arts. As a new instructor it felt easy to get lost. Often there was no deeper conversation beyond, "Okay, here's your class. You show up on this date. Bye." You were left to your own devices to think about important aspects such as: How do I teach? What does it mean to teach? We didn't want to repeat that for our own school. It's not good to have faculty who are really stressed out about wanting to teach learners but don't know how. We are trying to build more robust support structures for people who are new to the idea of facilitating a classroom environment. But we also have to acknowledge that there is so much labor that goes into that, and it might be invisible to the average person coming into a class on day one. That's one of the biggest challenges. How do we provide the best while also not burning out?

YE

To touch on what you're saying on the notion of an educator not being equipped properly in order to educate other learners, an alternative that we've been practicing and exploring for a while is called "peer apprenticeships." Peer apprenticeships are an opportunity for people to learn together and alongside one another without having an expectation of hierarchy. This is especially relevant in areas, or industries, where knowledge is emerging and there isn't already an established curriculum on how to teach it. Say, for example, someone has a friend that wants to learn how to sew, and that person has never sewn as well. They can have a peer apprenticeship together and figure out how they can get access to a sewing machine and learn from one another. That's a method that can be a potential solution for the situations in which educators may not be well equipped to provide the level of education that's expected from them.

LY

Regarding all of these new ways that you've been figuring out and exploring for learners and educators, would you say you're trying to create structures that you yourself didn't experience while you were a learner yourself in an institution?

YE

I would say it was first a learner's curiosity. Our curiosity brought us to hackathons and hackathons allowed us to learn alongside people from different schools. We would travel to different universities and spend the weekends learning how to make something with someone from a community college or an Ivy League. There was a diversity in the participant pool and a non-structure of curriculum that wasn't being offered at our school.

NO

Now it feels like we're creating educational environments that we wish we had and the educational environments that we want to be in. As educators, we're learning alongside learners about what this environment should be like. What should this circle of learning be? Or what should this school space be?

YE

People say, "Do what you love for work," but some people also don't have the circumstances to explore that. It's like therapy. We all go through emotions throughout the day and through our life and through the week, but our ability to articulate and digest them may not exist unless we put the time aside for that. Our relationship to work is something that we haven't as a society given enough time to examine and if we're able to better examine how we want to feel when we work, we may be better able to identify what environments we want to work in, with whom, and how.

An anecdote I can express is, as an example, my mother had me at a very young age. She does not have a high school degree but she runs a business. She's expressed that she wants to go to college multiple times throughout her life and that she always aspired to be in medicine, but her circumstances didn't really allow for that. She really upholds the value of a degree and instilled it in me. I wanted to drop out, and believe it would've been okay if I dropped out, but getting a degree was reassuring for her. Holding on to those old ways of thinking is a way that people are held back on what's possible. It's also a privilege to know what's possible today that was not before. People are able to career, as a verb, more than ever before because of technology. People who may not be as privileged may not be able to be aware of it because affordances for them aren't presented. It's about understanding what's possible more than anything else and understanding that education comes, as we've been talking about, in nontraditional forms.

LY

Being aware is a privilege in itself. Something that Juan and I talk about a lot because we have started running a scholarship, is the idea of even knowing that such opportunities exist can be a huge step up for a lot of folks.

Coming from a more traditional background in design, I think about how my education in New York City predominantly covered design of the United States and Europe. Nothing indigenous, nothing east of Germany. I consider myself to be someone who is trying to make education more inclusive, trying to diversify my curriculum and trying to have students of different backgrounds. Sometimes I have no idea if I'm doing anything right; I'm trying to do what I think is the best that I can be doing. At the same time, I admit that I had not experienced an education that I wanted to have, and so I'm making it up as I go. I'm trying to do my best but I don't have the answers, so I also invite other people to do their best. If we all just try to do our best, maybe we can figure something out together and have more hope for the future.

YE

We're all learners. We're peer apprenticing, from whatever distance, to figure out what's possible. And that hope allows us to look at things with optimism.

LY

What's next? Is there even a goal? Is the status of keeping on doing this on a daily, monthly, whatever basis, the goal in itself? What are our aspirations, our dreams?

NO

For me, it increasingly feels that learning, and educational environments, should be threaded throughout life and not just bundled into one short period of time and space. I'm thinking about learning environments that create other learning environments, becoming a cascading effect of new educational institution pop-ups for long enough to inspire others around them, and then they ramp down and others pop up. It just becomes a wave of educational institutions throughout one's life–whether we're growing up and we're toddlers learning how to walk, or we're trying to figure out how to make a living, or if you're building a family, or helping sustain a neighborhood.

LY

For now, my dream is, similar to what Norm just said, creating a little ecosystem. If we start something expecting it to grow into another big corporate-y institution, that is completely against the ethos of what I started. I want my initiatives to have a really good run, and want them to inspire other people to also do their own thing. I'm not super concerned in the long term whether I am doing something very specific. I want there to be little microcosms and communities of people doing their thing, and maybe we have this very wobbly looking Venn diagram where we all converge in the middle for some things. I dream of everything being a little bit more self-motivated and self-sustaining. People often struggle with the idea of starting something new because the first time doing something is difficult. But hopefully the next time another person wants to start something similar, it'll be easier. Maybe in some years we can sit back and just enjoy all the lovely communities that have sprung around us.

YE

Starting is good. Finishing is different. It may be equally as hard to understand what finished looks like, and understanding when something should end. Those conversations and realities may be harder to face, but something that gets overlooked is what comes with that. This composting can also be enriching for what comes next.

LY

Maybe in ten years we can have another conversation just like this, but about how we compost what we've done.

DIGITAL DIARY

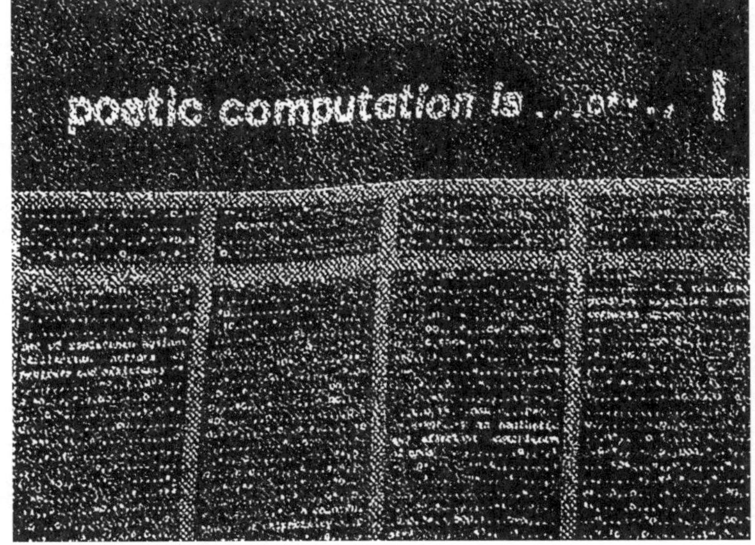

What is Poetic Computation?

Poetic computation's definition is ever blooming. We invite our participants to study in pursuit of both defining and resisting reductive expressions of poetic computation. These next few pages highlight written and visual definitions from alumni of the School for Poetic Computation.

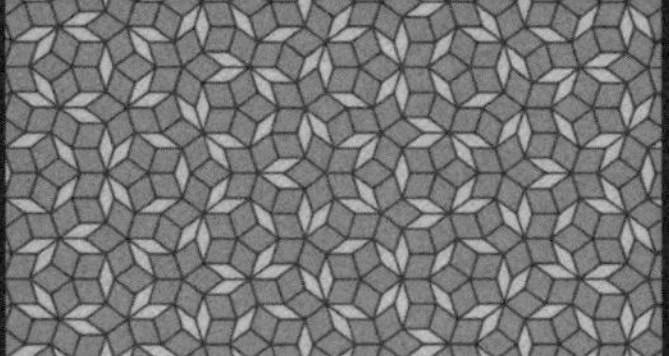

Poetic computation is a garden from where to play, learn, observe, and grow. *–Alberto Cuteri*

Poetic computation is dada with calculation. *–Beth O.*

Poetic computation is understanding the loving grace of seeing a machine eye-to-eye as equals rather than being watched over by them.
–Cam Morris

Poetic computation is the amalgamation of binary logic expressed in a human way.
–Camille Nibungco

Poetic computation is the feeling when you interact with machines, technology, software, hardware, screens, and devices that you are being embraced, that you are achieving what you'd like to achieve, or if you're not accomplishing precisely that (perhaps you don't know what should be done in the first place), then where you're being taken and what you find yourself doing is a wonderful unexpected gift.
–Charis P.

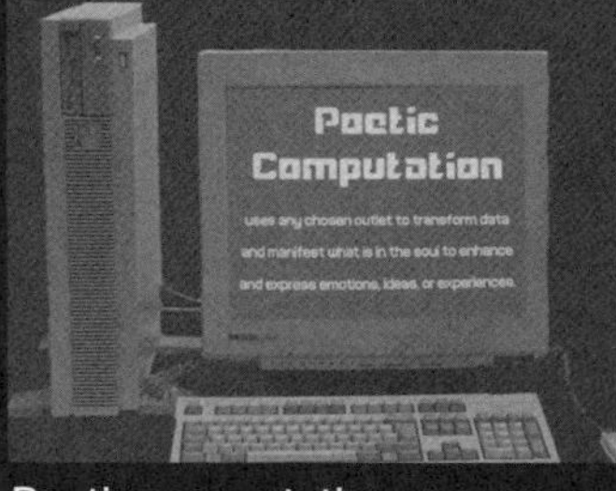

Poetic computation uses any chosen outlet to transform data and manifest what is in the soul to enhance and express emotions, ideas, or experiences.
–Chechi Amah

Poetic computation is the aftermath of a hike to the farthest limits one can find in computing and software, landing with a collection of memorabilia that speaks to the explorer on that journey.
–Erika Choe

For me, poetry, or rather, thinking poetically, is the only way we have to apprehend computation meaningfully. True, data is the mantra of our days; everything has a data dimension to it. Data is every bit of information we can get about, well, anything. ¶ It is true and is a reality that we need all that data, and all that data needs to be worked with. Data needs to be communicated, and in an easy way, among us, the humans. Our capacity is, however, limited, and the channels used to convey information have to be adapted. The main way through which we have communicated the unfathomable dimensions of our lives has been the way of the arts: dance, music, storytelling, images. And all of them have made use of one, simple, powerful device: the symbol. ¶ So complex is our data that it is difficult to apprehend. Unless symbolically. Or poetically if you wish. That hack of the language that is poetry, juxtaposing pieces in unusual context to entice our understanding in ways beyond our pedestrian routines. ¶ To be or not to be, that is the binary, pulsating, machine-level, electric question. Zero. One. Zero zero one. Zero one one. ¶ Data and symbol, or poetry, are therefore, two extremes of the same path; many times to go and come back between the two is difficult, but by being connected, both of them enrich exponentially: the data gets a powerful channel through where? I'm guessing that's what it should be... it can communicate its complexity, and the symbol gets a more tangible, feet-on-the-ground substance to its expressive power. *—german fernandez cantos*

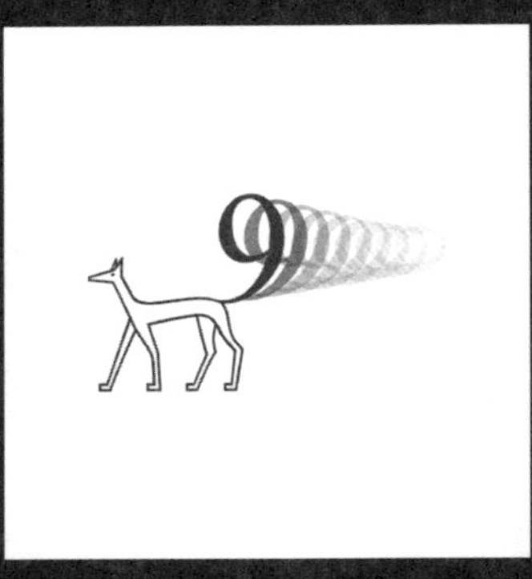

—Helen Shewolfe Tseng

embed glitches into ¶ tradition, imbue ways to ¶ know, grow — together *—hetvi*

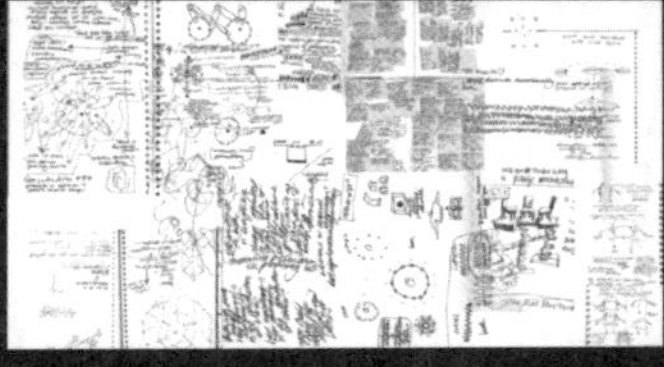

This collage is the result of seven years of compulsive note-taking turned into meticulous page-scanning, manipulated digitally to form new connections between disparate materials. The spaces between these subjects and forms are where I exist. *—Holly Adams*

Poetic computation is where tools meet ritual meet practice. *—Ilona Brand*

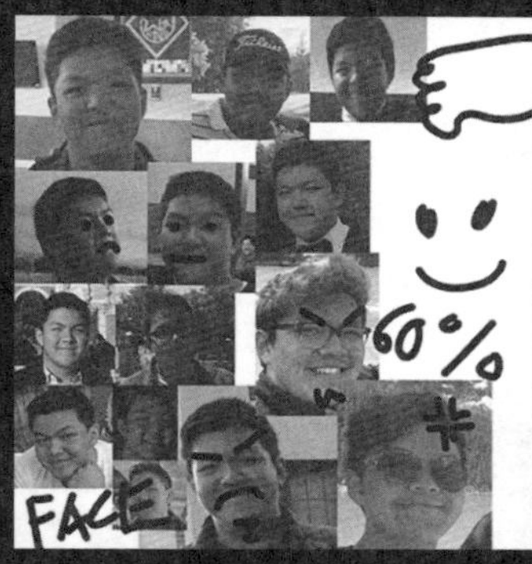

Poetic computation is the space that exists between formal logic and play. It asks us to understand the motivations of the world around us and subvert them. In a world driven by capitalist business logic, it posits: where is the humanity in these electrical builds? *–ivan zhao*

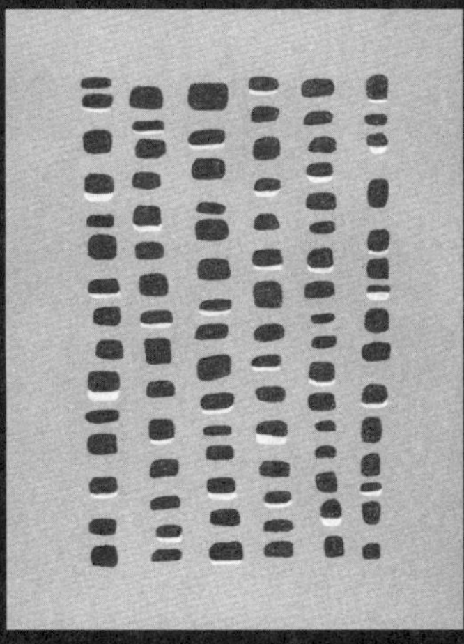

–Juan Miguel Marin

Poetic computation is the curation and act of networking an explication of human interactions with the environment, technology, others, or the self; hosting a gossamer, high-level projection of ideas, feelings, or experiences—a process that may exist as human and/or computer-aided intentions and instructions, transpiled to be in a low-level form most concrete through hardware or software mediums. *–Kate Grant*

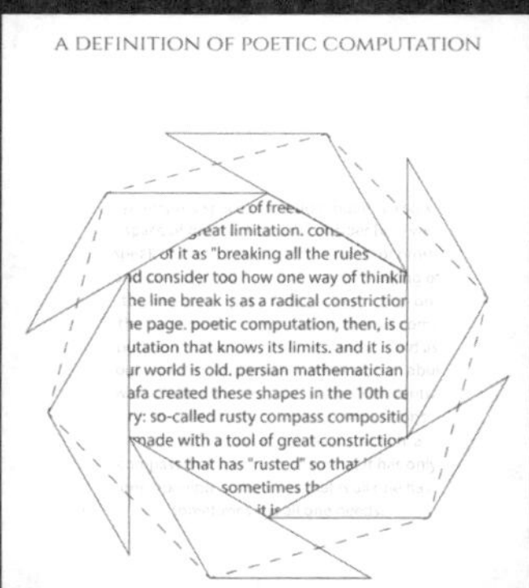
A DEFINITION OF POETIC COMPUTATION

–Keith S. Wilson

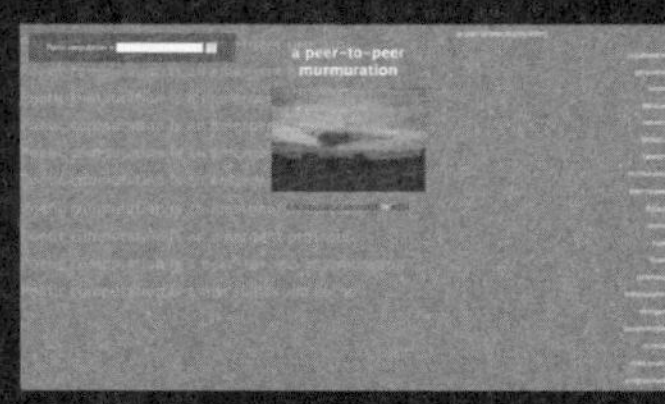

Poetic computation is an emergent protocol. *–Lauren St. Clair*

Poetic computation is when more happens in the mind than in the material world.
–Meghna Dholakia

Poetic computation is the formulation of perception, awareness, and delusion into stanzas—evoking the imagination in order to beautifully translate, and sometimes realize, the conceptual into actual. *—meghna mahadevan*

Poetic computation is the creative application of digital mechanic language for means that are revelatory, affective, and emancipatory. *—Mollie Burke*

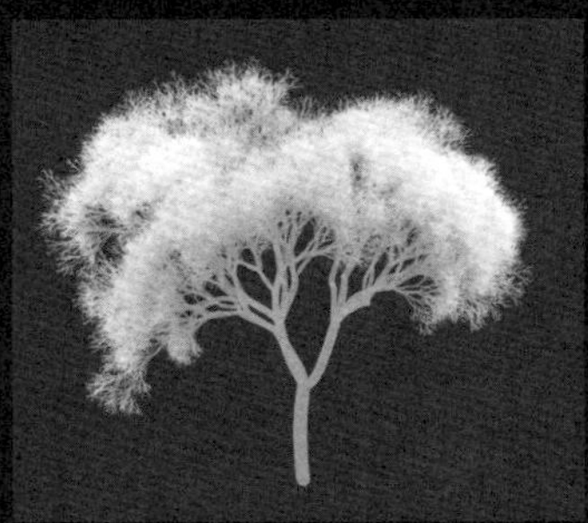

Poetic computation is the art of using rules to create feelings. *—N? Schager*

Poetic computation is a lyrical invocation to summon regenerative forces. As poetic computation unfurls, here, there, everywhere, it cultivates pathways to unlearn, to foster community and to reenchant. *—Nasrah Omar*

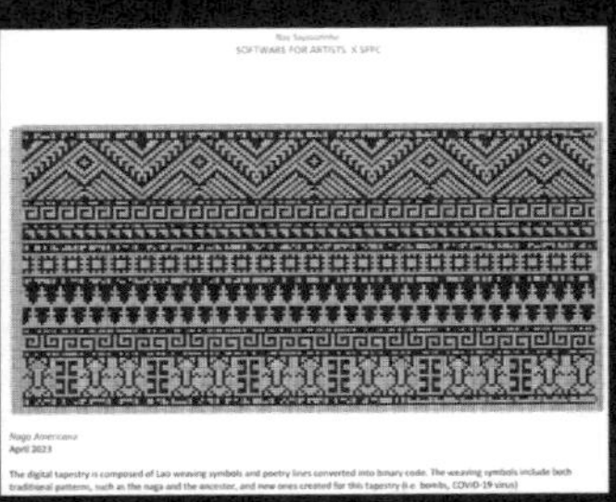

Computation expands our human ability to record and repeat all manner of things, but it is poetry that distills infinite archives into human memories. At the end of my life, I might no longer remember how a poem was meant to be constructed, yet it is the method of construction that will preserve a moment meant to be fleeting. ¶ This digital tapestry is composed of Lao weaving symbols and poetry lines converted into binary code. The weaving symbols include both traditional patterns, such as the naga and the ancestor, and new ones created for this tapestry (i.e., bombs, Covid-19 virus). *—Nay Saysourinho*

Poetic computation is a relational practice organized by communal study. *—Neta Bomani*

Poetic computation is the decoding, encoding, and experimentation with the codes/symbols/language of everyday life. *—Noelle Barrera*

–riley wong

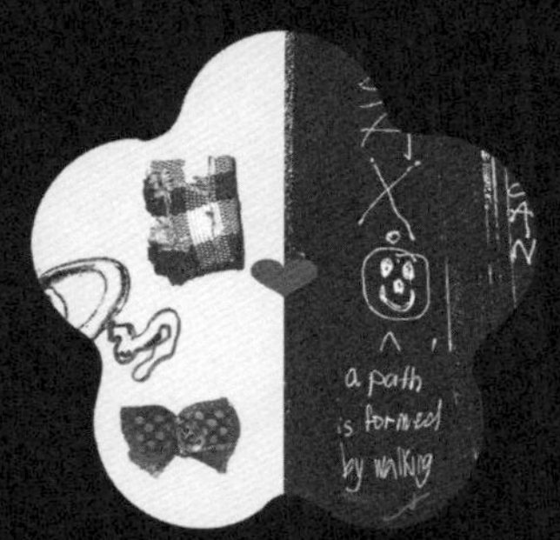

I always get my best ideas while walking around + looking down at the sidewalk in NYC. SFPC to me feels like a place that teaches people to take ideas like those seriously—no matter how far out, dreamy, and unfiltered they are, actually even going so far as to encourage them... This sticker is an ode to the free association that comes through this mode of thought and practice.
–Ritu Ghiya

= ¶ logic sings ¶ && ¶ reveals ¶
!= ¶ replicates ¶ ∴ ¶ worlds anew
–Riven Ratanavanh

Poetic computation is a conversation between operator and computer, an interaction with systems in which each piece has been caringly and deliberately coded. *–Romello Goodman*

Poetic computation brings a subversive whimsy to the financial and colonial logics that modern technologies are built directly on top of. ¶ If, as Baldwin says, "the poet or the revolutionary is there to articulate the necessity," the necessity that poetic computation seeks to articulate is the denaturalization of the diffuse yet all-encompassing techno-logics that continue to shape this reality. In other words, poetic computation sheds light on deeply ingrained capitalist and imperial mentalities ¶ in order to show how malleable our realities really are. *–samara alarcón*

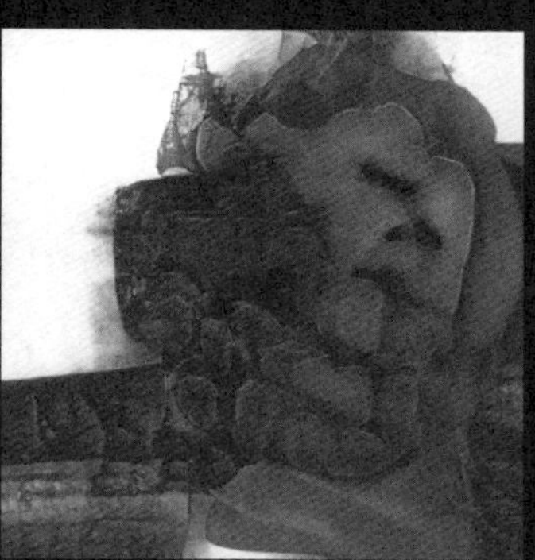

–Samuel Antonio Turner

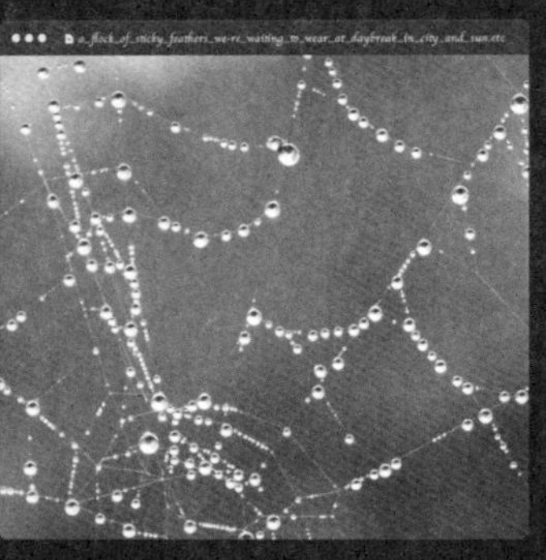

poetic computation is a letter for making love ¶ if i could, i'd whisk us to a realm of possibility that shimmers and sculpts our thighs, to a place where thoughts lead to modes of affection, where attention and affection are not products of an economy, not subject to a shortage of supply, not desperately demanded in the face of uncertainty, with sweat slowly dripping. i'd see you and kiss your fingertips before sending you off and patiently anticipating what need not be spoken into existence. ¶ poetic computation is a stream of thoughts on the futility of being self-aware ¶ lately, i've been thinking about notions of self-awareness, what we mean when we say we are "self-aware" or expect self-awareness in the people around us. and now i'm thinking about the expectations that are baked into a lot of daily interactions, how those expectations limit our ability to spend time with people and engage in our differing life patterns, and how we instead draw from our impressions of people (which are limited, formulaic, and informed by our impressions of ourselves). ¶ i'm thinking about how, when left unchecked, our expectations of each other can get entangled with our fragilities—the things we lack from within and desperately seek from without. this makes it difficult to see a person's boundaries in their true dimension, as healthy modes of expression that point to the threshold between a self and another connected self. ¶ i'm thinking about how, when left unattended, these expectations can very easily turn into a posture of entitlement . . . entitlement to the time, land, and labor of creatures and beings that don't belong to us, or anyone. ¶ it's a long and slow journey. ¶ poetic computation is a flock of sticky feathers we're waiting to wear at daybreak in city and sun, etc.
–*Shiraz Abdullahi Gallab*

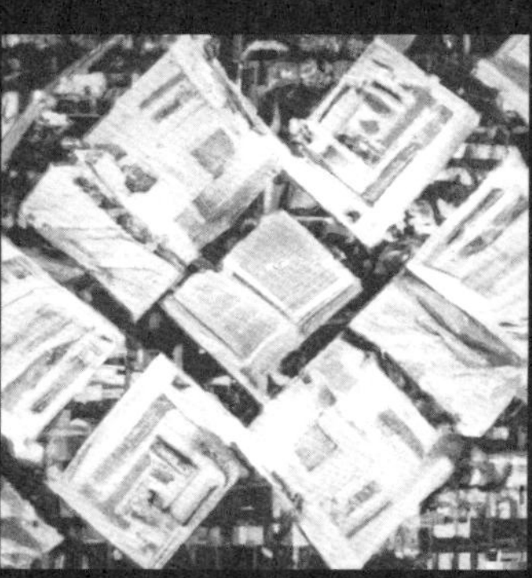

Poetic computation is where art and code unite, in a quest for truth and beauty, with fair tech as our guide, decolonization as our duty, and decentralization as our right.
–*Yanyi L.*

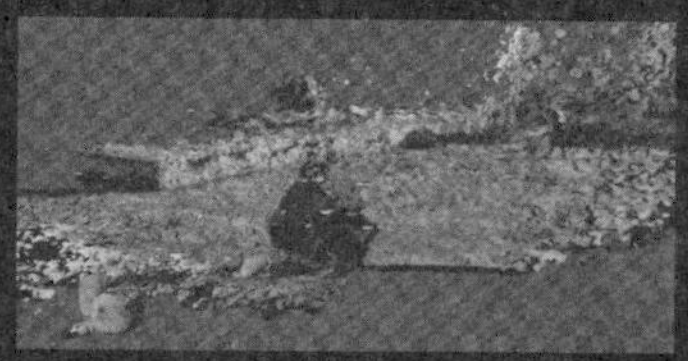

Poetic computation is to break engineers' hearts and blow artists' minds. *–Yufeng Zhao*